Sex, Lies, and the Truth

Sex, Lies, and the Truth
*Developing a Christian Ethic
in a Post-Christian Society*

LINDA L. BELLEVILLE

WIPF & STOCK · Eugene, Oregon

SEX, LIES, AND THE TRUTH
Developing a Christian Ethic in a Post-Christian Society

Copyright © 2010 Linda L. Belleville. All rights reserved. Except for brief quotations in critical publications or reviews, no part of this book may be reproduced in any manner without prior written permission from the publisher. Write: Permissions, Wipf and Stock Publishers, 199 W. 8th Ave., Suite 3, Eugene, OR 97401.

All Scripture quotations, unless otherwise indicated, are taken from the Holy Bible, New International Version®, NIV®. Copyright ©1973, 1978, 1984 by Biblica, Inc.™ Used by permission of Zondervan. All rights reserved worldwide. www.zondervan.com.

Wipf & Stock
An Imprint of Wipf and Stock Publishers
199 W. 8th Ave., Suite 3
Eugene, OR 97401

www.wipfandstock.com

ISBN 13: 978-1-60899-519-6

Manufactured in the U.S.A.

*To my son, Paul Raymond Belleville
and my daughter, Kathleen Renee Belleville*

Contents

Preface • ix

Abbreviations • xi

Introduction: The Dilemma • 1

ONE   The Casual-Sex Challenge • 7

TWO   The Marital Challenge • 29

THREE   The Same-Sex Challenge • 51

Conclusion: The Way Forward • 106

Bibliography • 115

Preface

I WISH TO EXPRESS my profound appreciation to Christian Amondson for accepting this volume in the Wipf & Stock imprint. It reflects two decades of research and writing, and of speaking to and interacting with people inside and outside the church.

I am deeply indebted to my tutorial assistant Thomas Kinnaird for his insightful reading and meticulous proofing of the book in draft form. I also wish to thank the students in my sexual ethics classes for their keen interaction and personal support during the final stages of the book's production—Gary Ingle, Jason Nelson, Anthony Parrott, Matt Metzger, Justin Ahlgrim, Jared Gregory, Sarah Thomas, Jon Baker, and David Poole.

This volume aims to bring the Bible to bear on an issue of central importance for the Christian life and of increasing complexity for the church's ministry. The book's intent is to help Christians in all walks of life become biblically informed and culturally conversant on a topic that promises to be one of the foremost challenges in the coming years. My hope is to provide a tool that is academically rigorous and pastorally relevant—a tool that stretches the mind and moves the heart to ever-growing faithfulness and obedience to our Lord and Savior, Jesus Christ.

Gloria Deo

Linda L. Belleville
Bethel College
April 15, 2010

Abbreviations

BIBLE TRANSLATIONS

ASV	American Standard Version
CEV	Contemporary English Version
DBY	Darby
ESV	English Standard Version
HCSB	Holman Christian Standard Bible
JB	Jerusalem Bible
KJV	King James Version
LXX	Septuagint
MRD	James Murdock Translation
NAB	New American Bible
NASB	New American Standard Bible
NASU	New American Standard Updated
NCV	New Century Version
NEB	New English Bible
NET	New English Translation
NIV	New International Version
NLT	New Living Translation
NKJV	New King James Version
NRSV	New Revised Standard Version
PNT	Bishop's New Testament
REB	Revised English Bible
RSV	Revised Standard Version
TEV	Today's English Version

TNIV	Today's New International Version
TNT	Tyndale's New Testament
WEB	The Webster Bible
YLT	Young's Literal Translation

ABBREVIATIONS OF STANDARD WORKS

BDAG	Walter Bauer, Frederick W. Danker, W. F. Arndt, and F. W. Gingrich. *Greek-English Lexicon of the New Testament and Other Early Christian Literature.* 3rd ed. Chicago: University of Chicago Press, 2000.
BDB	Francis Brown, S. R. Driver, and Charles A. Briggs. *Hebrew and English Lexicon of the Old Testament.* Oxford: Clarendon, 1907.
BDF	Friedrich Blass and Albert Debrunner. *A Greek Grammar of the New Testament and Other Early Christian Literature.* Translated and revised by Robert W. Funk. Chicago: University of Chicago Press, 1961.
LCL	Loeb Classical Library
L&N	J. P. Louw and E. A. Nida. *Greek-English Lexicon of the New Testament: Based on Semantic Domains.* 2 vols. New York: United Bible Societies, 1988–1989.
LSJ	Henry George Liddell, Robert Scott, and Henry Stuart Jones. *A Greek-English Lexicon.* 9th ed. With revised supplement. Oxford: Clarendon, 1996.
MM	James Hope Moulton and George Milligan. *The Vocabulary of the Greek Testament: Illustrated from the Papyri and Other*

	Non-Literary Sources. 1930. Reprinted, Peabody, MA: Hendrickson, 1997.
NICOT	New International Commentary on the Old Testament
P. Oxy.	B. P. Grenfell et al. *The Oxyrhynchus Papyri.* 42 vols. London: Egypt Exploration Fund, 1898–1974. http://www.papyrology.ox.ac.uk/POxy/VExhibition/images/2891.jpg.
TDNT	*Theological Dictionary of the New Testament.* 10 vols. Edited by Gerhard Kittel and Gerhard Friedrich. Translated by Geoffrey W. Bromiley. Grand Rapids: Eerdmans, 1964–1976.
TDOT	*Theological Dictionary of the Old Testament.* 14 vols. Edited by G. Johannes Botterweck and Helmer Ringgren. Translated by Geoffrey W. Bromiley et al. Grand Rapids: Eerdmans, 1974–2004.
TWOT	*Theological Wordbook of the Old Testament.* 2 vols. Edited by R. L. Harris, G. L. Archer, and B. K. Waltke. Chicago: Moody, 1980.
WBC	Word Biblical Commentary

ABBREVIATIONS OF THE PSEUDEPIGRAPHA AND OTHER ANCIENT SOURCES

As. Mos.	*Assumption of Moses*

Athenagoras

Leg.	*Legatio pro Christianis*

Josephus

Ag. Ap.	*Against Apion*
Ant.	*Antiquities*

Philo

Abr.	*On Abraham*
Spec. Laws	*On the Special Laws*

Sib. Or.	*Sibylline Oracles*

Testaments of the Twelve Patriarchs

T. Jos.	*Testament of Joseph*
T. Reu.	*Testament of Reuben*
T. Benj.	*Testament of Benjamin*

Introduction: The Dilemma

IN THE LAST THREE decades, society's attitudes toward casual sex, marriage and family, and same-sex relations have changed dramatically. The evidence for this is pervasive.

Casual sex between consenting adults scarcely gets a second look these days.[1] Billboards advertize it.[2] Retailers capitalize on it.[3] The media exploits it. It is the rare television show that does not have one or more characters involved in an extramarital relationship. In previous years, this was for the most part limited to afternoon programming and considered risqué. Now, extramarital relationships are a matter of prime-time viewing and thought to be normal and healthy.[4] The percentage of Americans

---

1. "Casual sex" is used in this volume in the strictest biblical sense of sexual intimacy outside of the bonds of marriage.

2. For example, a billboard on Interstate 355 through the western suburbs of Chicago solicits listeners for a local radio station by picturing its disc jockeys in the nude (sensitive anatomical parts blocked by hands, coffee cups, etc.).

3. American Eagle Outfitters markets and sells a line of clothing targeting fifteen- to twenty-five-year-olds. *Aerie* clothing is designed to be "sweetly sexy from the dorm room to the coffee shop to the classroom." It includes frisky thongs and boyfriend briefs for that "special guy in your life." Facebook page of American Eagle 756.

4. For instance, a female hospital administrator in a recent episode of *Royal Pains* expressed the opinion that a successful relationship is dependent upon determining sexual compatibility prior to tying the knot. *Royal Pains*, Season Two, Episode 1, June 4, 2010.

engaged in casual sex is alarming. This is especially the case regarding our youth. Recent polls indicate that about 50 percent of teenagers are sexually active.[5] It is therefore hardly surprising that the teenage pregnancy rate has tripled over the past thirty-five years, producing a society in which one child out of three is illegitimate.[6]

Attitudes toward marriage and family have also changed considerably. The number of singles has increased sevenfold.[7] Couples are marrying later, if at all. The number of never-married middle-aged men more than tripled, and the number of never-married women doubled over the last thirty-five years.[8] Failed marriages have become a fact of life, and couples are divorcing and remarrying in record numbers. In 1940, there were 264,000 divorces. By 1970 the number had tripled, and by 1996 it had quadrupled.[9] In addition, the trend is not merely to terminate a

5. U.S. Census Bureau, "Census 2000 Briefs"; National Survey of Family Growth.

6. Marilyn Gratton Kyd, "Baby Boomers Dreams Get Skunked," *Chicago Tribune*, November 28, 1995.

7. The number has increased from about .5 million in 1970 to 5 million today. U.S. Statistics, "Median Age at First Marriage"; U.S. Statistics, "Percent Never Married."

8. The number of households headed by unmarried heterosexuals has increased from 523,000 in 1970 to 4.9 million today. The number of never-married middle-aged men rose from 4.9 percent in 1970 to 17.6 percent in 2004. The number of never-married women doubled from 6.3 percent to 12 percent over the same time period. The median age for marriage has risen to twenty-five for women and twenty-seven for men. U.S. Statistics, "Percent Never Married"; Saluter and Lugaila, "Current Population Reports."

9. In 1940, there were 264,000 divorces. In 1970, the number jumped to 708,000. In 1996, divorces increased to 1,169,000. Since then, divorces have averaged between 1.1 and 1.2 million per year. U.S. Census Bureau, "Marriage and Divorce Data."

Introduction: The Dilemma

marriage, but to divorce and remarry one, two, even three or more times. Marriages are averaging 2.2 million per year, yet less than 50 percent are first marriages.[10]

Perhaps the most profound change has been in how Americans view the family. The family has been redefined in ways that challenge how we as Christians effectively minister to those inside and outside the church. Of the nation's family households, less than half have children present in the home.[11] Of households with children, the number of those with two parents has dropped significantly, while the number of single-parent households has correspondingly risen.[12] The result is that about one of every four families is currently maintained by a single parent. Even more striking is the fact that about 40 percent of these single parents are divorced, and another 35 percent have never married. The family has also become more complex than it once was. Children today are more likely to be living in a family that is not composed of two biological parents and full biological siblings—the traditional family of thirty-five years ago. They are more likely to have stepparents, stepbrothers, and stepsisters than ever before. A new twist in recent years is the rising number of two-parent families in which the parents are of the same

---

10. U.S. Census Bureau, "Statistical Abstract," section 2; Famighetti, "Vital Statistics," 962.

11. There are currently 105.5 million family households in the U.S.

12. Of these households, only 37 percent are families with two parents (compared with 50 percent two-parent families in 1970). The percentage of children under age eighteen living with two married parents fell from 77 percent in 1980, to 73 percent in 1990, 69 percent in 2000, and 67 percent in 2005. U.S. Census Bureau, "Census 2000 Briefs"; U.S. Statistics, "Households."

sex, and the children are either adopted or the product of impregnation by a third party (artificially or otherwise).[13] This increased social complexity is played out in the popular sitcom *Will & Grace*, which features a gay lawyer who fathers a boy with his lover through inseminating an opportunistic young lady, an interior designer who becomes pregnant with her ex-husband's baby after a one-night stand on an airplane, an alcoholic woman who is estranged from a wealthy husband jailed for tax fraud, and a gay actor who fathers a son through artificial insemination with a lesbian woman and marries an illegal immigrant to help her establish U.S. citizenship.

One of the most remarkable changes has been attitudes toward same-sex relationships. Thirty-five years ago, they were considered injurious and abnormal. Now same-sex relationships are commonly seen as acceptable and normal. Current media, including drama, comedy, cartoons, reality shows, and even game shows, reflects this attitudinal shift. In the mid-1990s, *Ellen* was the lone "coming out" television series. Now, virtually every sitcom has a gay or lesbian character.[14] High-profile lesbian roles in a prime-time television series number in the thirties, including new hit series and old favorites.[15] Gays fill prominent roles in new drama series and season premieres.[16]

---

13. U.S. Census Bureau, "Family and Living Arrangements."

14. See the ever-popular reruns of *Spin City*, *Friends*, *Grey's Anatomy*, and *Will & Grace*.

15. See the new hit series *The Good Wife* and old favorites such as *Nip/Tuck*.

16. See the new drama *Trauma* (with a gay paramedic) and the new season of *Law & Order: Special Victims Unit* (with a gay staff psychiatrist).

Introduction: The Dilemma

These shifting attitudes have presented a distinct challenge for the church. The dilemma is how to biblically and strategically engage them. Christians, both individually and corporately, have been slow to recognize their responsibilities. Some have uncritically absorbed and conformed to society's changes. Others have turned a blind eye so as not to offend in a society that idealizes toleration and political correctness. Still others have opted to condemn or simply to withdraw from society and its shifting mores.

If, however, we value our call to be the salt and light of the world (Matt 5:13–16) and we attach importance to our mission to "go and make disciples" (Matt 28:19), then acceptance, denial, mere condemnation, and withdrawal are not viable options. The first step is to become well versed in the changing sexual scene around us and conversant with the non-truths and half-truths used to justify current social mores. The next step is to become knowledgeable about the Bible's teaching regarding matters of sexual intimacy, singleness, marriage, and family. Then the task is to think strategically about the way forward in engaging those inside and outside the church.

As Christians and churches, we tend to shy away from talking about sex in a culture that has become virtually uninhibited on the topic. Yet the apostle Paul states that "we must grow up *in every way* into him who is the head, into Christ" (Eph 4:15 NRSV), and he puts sexual maturity at the top of the list (Eph 5:5). Such maturity occurs as we "speak the truth in love" and "as each member does its work by holding one another accountable in behavior and by building each other up in love" (Eph 4:16 AT). "So stop telling lies. Let us tell our neighbors the truth, for we are all parts of the same body" (Eph 4:25 NLT).

ONE

The Casual-Sex Challenge

TODAY'S SOCIETY IS FIXATED on sex. We are bombarded on a daily basis by a steady stream of it. Retailers capitalize on it: Victoria's Secret keeps setting the bar, but other retailers such as Abercrombie & Fitch and American Eagle Outfitters are not far behind.[1] Network television exploits it. Casual sex appears everywhere during prime-time viewing.[2] Sex fuels most popular young adult television series, and it is the rare comedy that does not abound in off-color jokes and sexually explicit language.[3] Even the dramas with serious themes include characters who constantly change sexual partners.[4]

---

1. Abercrombie & Fitch in the 1990s began peddling the worldview, "If you are not having sex, you are not having fun." The retailer's bags and ads with bare-chested college guys (appealing to both gays and gals) and video clips of topless girls (hands covering their breasts) draw junior and senior high shoppers by the thousands. See www.youthculture.com; www.abercrombie.com. For American Eagle, see http://www.ae.com/web/browse/category_aerie_guide.

2. "Casual sex" is used in this volume in the strictest biblical sense of sexual intimacy outside of the bonds of marriage.

3. See such shows as *Boston Legal* (ABC), *One Tree Hill* (CBS/CW, the *Dawson's Creek* successor), *Scrubs* (ABC), *Nip/Tuck* (Fox), *Two and a Half Men* (CBS), *The New Adventures of Old Christine* (CBS), and *Everybody Hates Christine* (the CW).

4. See, for example, *CSI*, *CSI Miami*, and *NCIS*.

Public media and government agencies assume most Americans are engaging in casual sex. Billboards warn men they can be spreading genital herpes and not know it; commercials advise women to "tell someone" that HPV causes cervical cancer.[5] The Centers for Disease Control and Prevention (CDC) claims that the U.S. has the highest rates of STDs of any industrialized country. Some 19 million new cases of a sexually transmitted disease are reported yearly. Approximately 20 million women are currently infected with the human papillomavirus (HPV). Another 100 thousand women are rendered infertile each year by the virus chlamydia.[6] HIV statistics are equally compelling. An estimated 1 million in the U.S. currently have the human immunodeficiency virus, with approximately 40 thousand new infections occurring each year.

Most people take for granted that teenagers are engaged in casual sex. Nearly half of reported STDs occur among young people. Of the twenty-nine sexually transmitted diseases identified by the National Board of Health, almost half of these occur among young people

---

5. "Tell Someone," the campaign of pharmaceutical company Merck & Co., launched in April 2006. In paid television ads, actresses expressed surprise about the cause of cervical cancer and promised to tell other women. Kaiser Health News, "FDA Announces Approval." Ads typically do not indicate that HPV is a sexually transmitted disease. CDC, "HPV Vaccine Information."

6. About 6.2 million women become newly infected with HPV each year. Women are typically infected in their teens, twenties, or thirties. The disease, however, can take up to twenty years to develop. Cervical cancer without surgery and radiation therapy can quickly progress to an invasive, fatal disease. HPV also causes sterility and genital warts. CDC, "Genital HPV Infection"; the National Institute of Allergy and Infectious Diseases, "Sexually Transmitted Infections." For statistics on chlamydia, see Kirchheimer, "Herpes Down."

ages fifteen to twenty-four.[7] Doctors' offices now routinely vaccinate eleven- and twelve-year-olds against HPV.[8] Although the dangers of casual sex are typically covered in health courses, the response of public schools has been to focus on having safe sex by using a condom.[9]

COMMON BELIEFS ABOUT CASUAL SEX

What accounts for these changing attitudes toward casual sex? A number of beliefs underlie them. The first is the belief that sex is an entitlement. In the 1960s, "sex makes free" was common as graffiti. Sex was viewed as a universal panacea for loneliness and human emptiness. Now sex is seen as a constitutionally guaranteed right, part of our inalienable right to life, liberty, and the pursuit of happiness. Thus, to say no to sex is to say no to personal happiness.

A second common belief is that casual sex is morally neutral. Sex is increasingly seen as doing what comes naturally. Fulfillment of sexual needs is put on a par with fulfillment of other bodily needs. Like sleeping and eating, sex is good nurture of the body. Sexual activity signals normality and health. If you don't indulge, you are labeled a prude or considered repressed.

---

7. CDC researchers estimate that one of every two new STDs diagnosed each year occurs in Americans between the ages of fifteen and twenty-four. Fifty percent of HIV infections each year occur among this age group. Thirty percent of those infected with HIV are women. CDC, "Trends in Risk Behaviors."

8. Doctors promote an HPV vaccine, and some suggest making Gardasil mandatory for females statewide. Stein, "Medical Groups Promoted Gardasil," 1–2.

9. "Condom Availability in High Schools," May 29, 2003, kaiserfoundation.org.

A third common belief is that casual sex is safe. Condoms have been presented as the "safe" option in public school curricula. As long as one takes the necessary precautions, what is the harm? To this end, Joycelyn Elders, the U.S. Surgeon General during the Clinton administration, advocated installing condom machines in our public school bathrooms.[10]

THE REALITIES ABOUT CASUAL SEX

The reality is that casual sex is not good nurture and doing what comes naturally. Reports show that sexually active women are more likely to be clinically depressed, have low self-esteem, feel lonely, or attempt suicide.[11] Sexually active teenagers are more prone to substance abuse and more inclined to have trouble in school than those who are not active.[12] Also, the language of "protected" sex glosses over the health risks. Although condoms are perceived to be a "safe" option, the reality is otherwise. It has long been documented that condoms have a 15 percent annual failure rate in protecting against pregnancy and provide no guarantee against STDs.[13] Oral sex, pornography, phone

10. Janet Elliott, "Ex-Surgeon General: Condoms, Not Promises, Help Teens," *Houston Chronicle*, May 20, 2008, http://www.ripnroll.com/surgeon-general.htm.

11. Laura Vanderkam, "Sexually Active Girls' Lament: Why Didn't I Wait?" USA Today, June 6, 2003, http://www.usatoday.com/news/opinion/editorials/2003-06-11-vanderkam_x.htm.

12. Radsch, "Teenagers' Sexual Activity," A15; Orr et al., "Premature Sexual Activity," 141–47.

13. Information about the risks of condom use has been available for some time. Slippage, breakage and leakage are common problems. Elise Jones and Forrest, "Contraceptive Failure Rates," 12, 18; Gordon, "Critical Review," 5–30.

sex and cybersex are sometimes presented as safe alternatives, but the consequences of these are equally troubling.[14] Technology has provided many more opportunities for casual sex. The Internet has become an ideal medium for advertising and promoting sex parties, circuit parties, raves, local prostitution, and public and commercial sex venues. MySpace and Facebook have become the social networks of choice. Alcohol and drugs, which are present in abundance in such venues, have their own risks. Ecstasy and crystal methamphetamine have become the drugs of choice. Beyond eliminating inhibitions, ecstasy and meth are established contributors to reckless behavior, forgetfulness, blackouts, dizziness, respiratory problems, and brain damage.[15]

The National Coalition for Abstinence Education has pressured the federal government to do something about sexual promiscuity. In 1996, Congress allocated $250 million in state funding over five years to promote abstinence as an alternative health-education track in the public schools.[16] In addition, abstinence language has now found its way onto government websites. The

---

14. The fact is that oral sex carries the same STD risks, including the transmission of HPV, herpes, and HIV viruses and consequent oral ulcers, hepatitus B, and oral cancers. CDC, www.cdc.gov/mmwr/preview/mmwrhtml/mm5341a2.htm.

15. "Drugs, Doses & Effects," Healthcommunities.com.

16. The program was renewed in 2002 as Title V legislation, but opposition has been fierce. Sexuality Information and Education Council, "Knowing the Opposition." As of July 2008, only twenty-eight states utilized federal funds for abstinence education. Of the $50 million budgeted for the program this past year, only $21 million has been distributed. Law Students for Reproductive Justice, "Abstinence-Only Education."

CDC states: "The surest way to avoid transmission of sexually transmitted diseases is to abstain from sexual intercourse, or to be in a long-term mutually monogamous relationship with a partner who has been tested and you know is uninfected."[17] The church, for its part, has addressed the prevalence of casual sex among teens through support and intervention groups such as True Love Waits, Project Reality, and Teen-Aid.

During the last decade, abstinence-promotion efforts resulted in a 16 percent decrease in sexual activity among high school students and a 24 percent decline in the number of teens who have sex with multiple partners.[18] These statistics are encouraging, but more needs to be done. The church has yet to address the root causes of shifting sexual mores in substantive and strategic ways. The first step is to familiarize ourselves with the relevant biblical teaching.

THE NEW TESTAMENT PERSPECTIVE ON CASUAL SEX

It is a common perception that attitudes toward sex in the twenty-first century are unlike those of the first century. Yet, even a cursory look at the NT shows that first-century believers struggled with the same casual attitudes toward sex as we do. A clear tip-off is the fifty-five times the noun *porneia* ("sexual immorality") and related terms appear. Paul, in particular, had to tackle the topic in virtually

17. CDC, "Male Latex Condoms."

18. See Robert Rector, "The Effectiveness of Abstinence Education Programs in Reducing Sexual Activity Among Youth," *Backgrounder* #1533, April 8, 2002, http://www.heritage.org/Research/Reports/2002/04/The-Effectiveness-of-Abstinence-Education-Programs.

every letter he wrote to his churches.[19] This undoubtedly was because of the sexual license he encountered in the non-Jewish contexts in which he ministered.

Wherever one turns in the NT, there is an unequivocal rejection of *porneia*. Jesus defined the term as "evil things" that come from within and "defile a person" (Mark 7:21–23; Matt 15:15–20 NRSV). The Jerusalem church identified it as one of four activities that rendered Jew–Gentile fellowship impossible (Acts 15:20–29). The author of Hebrews names it as something God most certainly will judge (Heb 13:4), and Jude speaks of those who give themselves up to it as an example of those who suffer the punishment of eternal fire (Jude 7).

But what is meant by *porneia*? What all is included? Originally the word group referred just to prostitution.[20] By NT times, however, it included much more. Jewish literature close to the NT period included under the umbrella of *porneia* such activities as casual sex (*As. Mos.* 2.5), sexual solicitation (Sir 9:6–7),[21] adultery (Sir 23:17–18, 23),[22] incest (Sir 23:17; *T. Reu.* 1.6), religious prostitution (Wis 14:12; Sir 36:11), and same-sex practices (Josephus, *Ag. Ap.* 2.199; Philo, *Abr.* 135–136).[23] Jesus' use of the plural, sexual immoralities, suggests a similar range of mean-

---

19. Rom 1:18–27; 1 Cor 5:1, 9–11; 6:9, 13, 15–16, 18; 7:2; 10:8; 2 Cor 12:21; Gal 5:10, 19; Eph 5:3, 5; Col 3:5; 1 Thess 4:3; 1 Tim 1:10; compare Acts 15:20, 29; Heb 13:4.

20. The *porn-* word group includes *porneuō*, *pornē*, *pornos*, and *ekporneuō*.

21. Compare Hos 1:2 LXX.

22. Compare Wis 14:26; Philo, *Abr.* 135–136; *T. Jos.* 3.8.

23. Compare *T. Benj.* 9.1; *Sib. Or.* 2.73.

ings (Mark 7:21; Matt 15:19). And Paul speaks of *cases* of sexual promiscuity (1 Cor 7:2).

In the NT, one finds *porneia* used of casual sex (John 8:41; 1 Cor 7:1–2; 1 Thess 4:3; Heb 12:16), adultery (Matt 5:32; 19:9; 1 Cor 6:9; 1 Tim 1:10; Heb 13:4), sexual solicitation (Matt 21:31–32; Luke 15:30; 1 Cor 6:15–18), religious prostitution (Rev 2:14, 20), male prostitution (1 Cor 6:9), same-sex activity (Rom 1:27; 1 Cor 6:9; 1 Tim 1:10), and incest (1 Cor 5:1). In short, the NT writers label any extramarital or same-gender sexual activity as *porneia,* that is, sexual immorality.

PAUL'S SEX 101

Even though there are numerous NT references to sexual activity (both appropriate and inappropriate), there is little systematic teaching on the topic. In part, this is because sexual instruction was a core component of the teaching new believers received. At several points Paul reminds his converts of the instructions he had given them "by the authority of the Lord Jesus" (1 Cor 7:2). These periodic reminders help us reconstruct the basics of Paul's "Sex 101" instruction.

First, abstention from *porneia* is not an option but a requirement of holy living. Paul tells the Thessalonian believers: "It is God's will that you should be sanctified: that you should avoid sexual immorality" (1 Thess 4:3). Though the NIV translates the verb *apechesthai* as "avoid," the meaning is actually closer to "have nothing to do with." Moderation is not enough; only complete abstinence will do. And this comes as a command, not as a suggestion. It is *God's will* and his "marching orders" for all believers.[24]

---

24. The Greek term *parangelia* refers to the commands military leaders give their troops.

Second, a life of *porneia* is incompatible with membership in God's kingdom. Paul does not mince words. "You know perfectly well," he says, "that people who do wrong will not inherit the kingdom of God" (1 Cor 6:9 JB). This includes the sexually promiscuous, idolaters, adulterers, male prostitutes, and those who engage in same-sex practices (1 Cor 6:9–10; cf. Eph 5:5). The language of "inheriting the kingdom of God" is specific to Jesus' teaching. This is an important point. Too often it is assumed that Paul's uncompromising stance is a byproduct of his own inexperience and native prejudice against physical intimacy. Instead, the language points to a code of ethics adopted by the church early on and passed along to all church plants (cf. Acts 15:29).

Third, *porneia* is nowhere written off as a slight and understandable indiscretion. It is consistently placed first among sinful activities: "The acts of the sinful nature are obvious: sexual immorality, impurity, debauchery" (Gal 5:19–21); "Put to death whatever belongs to your earthly nature: sexual immorality, impurity, lust" (Col 3:5). Sexual sin is not something God ignores or merely scolds; it warrants nothing less than his judgment. "Because of these," Paul states, "the wrath of God is coming" (Col 3:6). The author of Hebrews echoes this warning: "God will judge the adulterer and all the sexually immoral" (Heb 13:4).

Fourth, sexual sin has a way of so overpowering and controlling a person's life that nothing less than its complete eradication will suffice. That is why Paul commands the Colossian believers to "put to death" sexual immorality, impurity, and lust and instructs the Corinthians to "flee" from any temptation to act out sexually (1 Cor 6:18). It is also why he tells them not to associate with anyone who claims to be a Christian and yet is sexually promiscuous. One is not even to eat with such a person (1 Cor 5:9–11).

THE NEED FOR A REFRESHER COURSE

At times the allure was just too great for the first-century Christian, and the simple command to "flee" from sexual temptation did not suffice. What then? What was the next step? Paul's letters to the Corinthian church are a response to this very situation. They provide a helpful insight into what a refresher course on sex looks like. In the Corinthian congregation, the sexual challenges included an incestuous affair between a member of the congregation and a non-Christian family member and the men purchasing the sexual favors of local prostitutes (1 Cor 5:1–13; 6:12–20).

The way Paul handles the matter of incest is particularly instructive because it is an instance where the local church dropped below the sexual standards of its society: "It is actually reported that there is sexual immorality among you, and of a kind that does not occur even among the pagans: A man has his father's wife" (1 Cor 5:1). In short, a member of the Corinthian church was having a sexual affair with his stepmother. That this was not a one-time lapse is indicated by the present-tense Greek verb "is living with" (NRSV). The fact that the man is the only one named as culpable indicates that the woman was not a Christian. The phrase "his father's wife," rather than "his mother," shows that the woman involved was not a blood relative. It also seems that the man's father was either divorced or deceased; otherwise Paul would have named the sexual offense "adultery" (*moicheia*).

The Casual-Sex Challenge

Twenty-first century readers might not see this as a case of incest. After all, the woman was not the man's biological mother. Yet OT Mosaic law clearly prohibited it: "Do not have sexual relations with your father's wife" (Lev 18:18). Mosaic law was concerned to establish boundaries within which a man may seek a wife for himself, and a child–stepparent relationship was not permissible. Roman law prohibited it as well. Cicero is representative in calling such a state of affairs "unbelievable" and "unheard of in all human experience" (Cicero, *In Defense of Cluentius* 15). The prohibition was based on the idea of relatedness by clan adoption.

Although a stepmother would not have been a blood relative, marriage made her an integral and permanent part of the family in a fashion that is largely foreign to Western thinking today.[25] Yet, it was very much a part of Greco-Roman thinking in the first century. Hence, Paul's comment that such a relationship was "not found even among non-Jews" (1 Cor 5:1).

Yet, the Corinthian believers were "proud" of this relationship. They did not turn a blind eye to it or even try to sweep it under the carpet. Instead, they wore it as a badge of freedom. "All things are lawful for me," they claimed (1 Cor 6:12 NRSV). "Sex is my right"—a claim not all that different from social attitudes today. But that it should surface in the church is quite surprising.

---

25. See Wenham, *Leviticus*, 253–55; Conzelmann, *1 Corinthians*, 96 n. 29.

THE NEED FOR DISCIPLINE

Paul identifies the appropriate congregational response to the flouting of social mores. In the first place, the Corinthian church should have been "filled with grief" (*epenthēsate*; 1 Cor 5:2a). The idea is not merely to be sad about something, but to grieve with the grief one feels over the death of a loved one. In the second place, the church should have put the offender out of its fellowship ("expelled from your midst" 5:2b NAB). Even now Paul calls the church to "expel the wicked man" from among them and to "hand him over to Satan" so that "the flesh" can be destroyed but "his spirit" saved (1 Cor 5:12; 5:5). These phrases show the seriousness with which casual sex should be viewed. Its gravity stems from the devastating consequences of such a lifestyle on the church's life and witness.

Discipline is difficult in the best of circumstances, but it is necessary for two reasons. First, the purity of the congregation is at risk. As Paul puts it, "A little yeast works through the whole batch of dough," or as we say today, "One bad apple spoils the barrel" (1 Cor 5:6). We tend to think that if someone else can do something, we can too—especially if the person holds a church leadership position. We forget that the church is Christ's bride-to-be and is to remain chaste until his return (2 Cor 11:1–2; Eph 5:27; Rev 21:9). In Paul's day, a father jealously guarded his daughter's purity until the day of her marriage. Church leaders are similarly to guard the church's purity and must therefore remain "above reproach" themselves (1 Tim 3:2, 10; Titus 1:6).

Second, discipline is necessary so as not to compromise the church's witness: "We put up with anything," states Paul, "rather than hinder the gospel of Christ" (1 Cor 9:12). One danger of living in a non-Christian world is becoming conformed to the world's standards rather than being transformed by God's standards. It is a particular danger for any church that takes pride in its freedom and tolerance. When the local church looks no different than society, it ceases to be salt and light to those around it. Quite often this happens imperceptibly, and the church becomes acculturated without even recognizing it. If it falls below the social norms of the day, as the Corinthian church did, it is truly harmful for the gospel witness.

THE NEED FOR SOUND THEOLOGY

A second sexual concern Paul faced was church men purchasing sexual favors from the local prostitutes. He writes, "Shall I take the members of Christ and unite them with a prostitute?" (1 Cor 6:15). The way the Corinthians justified their conduct was not unlike the way some believers justify such behavior today. The theological term commonly used of this way of thinking is "libertine." The logic is quite simple: The material world is destined for destruction. As such, it and everything related to it is of no account. It is the spiritual that endures, so it alone is valuable in the overall scheme of things. Grow your spiritual life; it matters. What you do with your body, however, does not matter. As we say, "earth to earth, ashes to ashes, dust to dust."[26] This places the body in the realm of *adiaphora*, or matters

26. Book of Common Prayer, "Burial of the Dead: Rite Two," 501.

of moral indifference. To indulge one's sexual appetite is no different from indulging other physical appetites such as eating and sleeping. In the final analysis, spiritual things are what count. The physical belongs to a passing age and hence is of no value.

Paul's response in 1 Cor 6:12–20 is important because it is the closest he comes to articulating a biblical theology of sexual intimacy. He presents five truths at odds with the libertine view.

First, our bodies are not destined for destruction but for resurrection: "By his power God raised the Lord from the dead, and he will raise us also" (1 Cor 6:14). Contrary to libertine thinking, our bodies are not part of this transient world order; they are destined for salvation. Therefore, what we do with our bodies is of the highest moral value.

Second, commitment to Christ involves the whole person, which includes our physical body. Paul asks, "Do you not know that your bodies are members of Christ?" (1 Cor 6:15). He goes on to describe this commitment as a union that makes the two, one. In a bold move, Paul takes a text normally applied to marriage ("the two will become one flesh") and applies it to our union with Christ: "the one who cleaves to the Lord is one with him in spirit" (Gen 2:24; 1 Cor 6:17).

To engage in sexual intimacy, Paul says, is to forge a union between two people. The problem is that an intimate, union with Christ already exists. So we are not free to take what belongs to Christ and give it to another. When we say "I do" to Christ at conversion, an intimate union is formed. All other unions must therefore be compatible with this most basic of unions. This is what is wrong with all extramarital sexual relationships—be they casual, adulterous, same-sex, incestuous, bestial, or premarital. They are not true unions. The only sexual activity that is compatible with our union with Christ is sexual activity within the context of marriage. This is because marriage alone is a divinely ordained institution. It is "what God has joined together" and what he alone has the authority to "split apart" (Mark 10:9; Matt 19:6 NLT).

Third, sexual sin impacts the body in a way other sins do not. Paul writes, "All other sins people commit are outside their bodies, but those who sin sexually sin against their own bodies" (1 Cor 6:18 TNIV). At first glance, this is a confusing claim. What about drinking, smoking, gluttony, or self-mutilation? Are these not also sins committed against one's own body? Yet, while there are, to be sure, other self-inflicted wrongs, sexual sins strike at what is intrinsic to our humanness in a way that the others do not. As one commentator notes, there is no other sin that so directly wounds our personal dignity and affects our self-esteem.[27] There is no act more intimate, that renders one as personally vulnerable, as sexual intimacy. To engage in sex apart from the public exchange of vows that promise a lifelong and exclusive commitment is to put oneself and one's union with Christ at tremendous risk.

Fourth, our body is not only destined to be raised with Christ, but even now it is the sphere of God's redemptive activity: "Do you not know that your body is the temple of the Holy Spirit?" (1 Cor 6:19). The term Paul uses is actually the *naos*, "inner sanctuary," of the Holy Spirit (not *hieron*, "temple"). In Jesus' day this inner sanctuary was located in what was considered a magnificent architectural

---

27. Allo, *Seconde Epitre aux Corinthiens*, 149.

structure (Mark 13:1). Now, this inner sanctuary is located in human flesh. What Jesus' death and resurrection made possible is God's presence in us through his Spirit. It is his indwelling Spirit that forges that union with Christ at conversion, making our bodies members of Christ himself (1 Cor 6:15, 17).

Fifth, our bodies are not ours to do with as we please; they belong to Christ. Paul states, "You are not your own; you were bought at a price" (1 Cor 6:19b–20). He writes elsewhere that the Spirit "anoints" us and "sets God's seal of ownership on us" until Christ returns (2 Cor 1:24). Americans often talk about their rights and freedoms to do as they please. In reality, however, this kind of freedom is an illusion. Paul's language is that of the marketplace, where slaves are bought and sold. It points to the reality that we all serve some master. If we give in to our sexual urges, we become their slave while they become our master. Sexual sin is addictive. It enslaves, whether mentally or physically. Paul tells the Corinthians, "You may say, 'I am allowed to do anything.' But I reply, 'Not everything is good for you.' And even though 'I am allowed to do anything,' I must not become a slave to anything" (1 Cor 6:12 NLT). We are free to choose what or whom to serve. We can chose to serve Christ, the only rightful master, or we can chose to serve our sinful urges.

SEX AND LUST

What about matters of lust? It is often said that the Bible does not address an enlightened, postmodern society such as ours. "We are enlightened about such matters. Biblical times were the dark ages. They didn't know that boys will be boys and girls will be girls at the onset of puberty"—so current rationalization goes. However, human nature is human nature, regardless of the date and place. Lustful looks, impure thoughts, coarse language, and lewd behavior know no temporal or cultural boundaries. They were as much of a challenge in NT times as in ours.

That lust is an ancient problem is evident from the wide range of sexual vices beyond *porneia* that surface in the "do-not" lists of the NT. The challenges include impure thoughts (*akatharsia*; 2 Cor 12:21; Gal 5:19; Eph 4:19; 5:3; Col 3:5; 1 Thess 4:7), lust (*epithymia*; Matt 5:28; Rom 1:24; Col 3:5; 1 Thess 4:5), covetous thoughts (*pleonexia*; Eph 5:3; Col 3:5), and lewd acts (*aselgeia*; 2 Cor 12:21; Gal 5:19; Eph 4:19). Jesus addressed them; they comprise virtually half of all the vices Paul lists; and every church plant received teaching about them.

What form did these vices take in the first century? Were they comparable to the sexual vices of today? "Impure thoughts" are ones that are "filthy" or "dirty" and would include what we call pornography today.[28] "Lust" is imagining or fantasizing about sexual intimacy with another person. It includes undressing someone with your eyes or thinking, *She's a babe. He's a stud.* "Lewd" behavior (*aselgeia*) is that which is lacking in moral restraint—indecent exposure, sexually explicit public gestures or speech, orgies, and the like. The preponderance of such behaviors was as much a part of first-century Western society as it is nowadays. Every NT document addresses

---

28. L&N, ἀκαθαρσία, §79.54: (1) any substance that is filthy or dirty; (2) a sexual vice or indecency (e.g., Rom 1:24).

them, which means every first-century church struggled with them.

While some today concede that casual sex has its dangers, many consider a lustful thought or look to be no big deal. Indeed, some see lustful thoughts and sexual fantasies as a safety mechanism. Better to think about the deed than to do it. Justifications include, "It doesn't hurt anyone," "It is the way guys are wired," and "Everybody does it, so it must be OK."[29]

Jesus, however, thought sexual fantasies were a big deal. And he calls those who would follow him to a standard of conduct that includes even our thought life. Jesus taught his followers that "any man who looks at a woman to lust after her has already committed adultery with her in his heart" (Matt 5:28). Lust, according to Jesus, is the same as premarital sex. It is the equivalent of defrauding a woman's future spouse by stealing her virginity—enjoying a physical intimacy (whether actual or imagined) that belongs to another. Sexual thoughts are to be only for one's spouse, present or future. That is where the battle lies today, and it is where the battle lay in past days. Job 31:1–8 reflects a similar standard, showing that lust is a common human struggle: "I made a covenant with my eyes not to look lustfully at a girl ... If my steps have turned from the path, if my heart has been led by my eyes, or if my hands have been defiled, then may others eat what I have sown, and may my crops be uprooted."

What Jesus himself recognized, and what he calls believers to recognize, is that *porneia* begins in the mind.

29. See WebMD, "Modern Love"; Genung, "How Many Porn Addicts?" Support groups include Pure Warrior Ministries (www.purewarrior.org) and Crosswalk.com.

Lustful thoughts must be nurtured for anything in the physical realm to occur. This is why he told his disciples to do whatever it takes to stop lustful thinking and sexual fantasizing. Jesus likens this vigilance to plucking out the offending eye or cutting off the offending hand (Matt 5:29–30). The metaphor is easily understood: to prevent the spread of a malignant growth, surgical removal is required

The standard of sexual purity Paul calls for is equally high. He tells the Colossian believers to "put to death" what is earthly in them: sexual immorality (*porneia*), filthy thoughts (*akatharsiai*), lustful fantasies (*epithymiai*), and covetous relationships (*pleonexiai*). Such, he asserts, are forms of "idolatry" and will exclude a person from any "inheritance in God's kingdom" (Col 3:5; Eph 5:5). There "must not be even a hint" of such thoughts or behaviors—whether it be a promiscuous action, an impure thought, or a covetous deed (Eph 5:3). In writing to the Galatian churches, he states, "the works of the flesh are plain," including "sexual immorality, filthy thoughts, and lewd acts" (Gal 5:19). He warns the Corinthian church that he will discipline any and all who have not repented of such thoughts and behaviors (2 Cor 12:21). And he reminds the Thessalonian believers that God has not called us to think "filthy thoughts" but "holy ones" (1 Thess 4:7)

Paul describes the society in which he lived as "futile" in its thinking, "darkened in its understanding," and "separated from the life of God" (Eph 4:17–18). What caused him to make this judgment was the observation that people of his society had become callous and had given themselves up to lewd acts, greedy to put every filthy thought into practice, with a continual lust for more (Eph 4:19). Rather than imitate the world, believers are called instead to imitate God and to live a life of self-denial, just as Christ did. There must not be anything that smacks of self-indulgence—including "obscenities, foolish talk, or coarse joking," which are totally out of place and mark a person who engages in them as "an idolater" (Eph 5:3–5). As far as the world goes, God had long since "given humanity up in the lusts of their hearts ... to the degrading of their bodies among themselves" (Rom 1:24 NRSV). This is because self-indulgence is at heart idolatry, "worship[ping] and serv[ing] created things rather than the Creator" (Rom 1:25).

Paul's language of futile thinking, darkened understanding, and separation from God explains why lustful looks, coarse language, and lewd behavior are such big deals: They damage us and damage others. They indulge self at the expense of another. They dehumanize another by making that person merely the object of sexual gratification. To undress someone with your eyes reduces who they are to how they look.

Lust is also psychologically damaging to those who indulge in it. Thought patterns easily become habitual; what we regularly think about can become an obsession. The images with which we fill our minds are difficult to erase, which is why pornography is so addictive. Whether virtual or actual, lustful thoughts and behaviors enslave. Studies indicate that 40 million U.S. adults regularly visit Internet pornography websites. Ten percent of adults admit to Internet sexual addiction, while 20 percent of men admit to accessing pornography at work. Those who self-identify as Christians appear particularly prone. Forty-seven percent of those surveyed said pornography was a major problem in the home, even as fifty-three percent of Promise Keepers said they had viewed pornography in the past week.[30]

The mind, the world of our thoughts, is Satan's front line of attack. To win the mind is to win the battle. Satan has "blinded the minds of unbelievers, so that they cannot see the light of the gospel of the glory of Christ, who is the image of God" (2 Cor 4:4).

The mind was also Paul's front line of attack. His job was to "take captive every thought to make it obedient to Christ" (2 Cor 10:5). This is why he commands us to "fix [our] thoughts on what is true and honorable and right, and pure, and lovely, and admirable. Think about things that are excellent and worthy of praise" (Phil 4:8 NLT). Obedience to Christ requires a renewal of our mind (Rom 12:2). Jesus prayed to the Father, "Not what I will, but what you will" (Mark 14:36). We can confidently pray, "Not what I *think* but what Christ *thinks*," for "we have the mind of Christ" (1 Cor 2:16).

In the final analysis, sexual purity is not an option. Whether we are unmarried or divorced, have a significant other, or are engaged, we are commanded as believers to

---

30. A 1996 Promise Keepers survey at one of their stadium events revealed that over 50 percent of the men in attendance had been involved with pornography within one week of attending the event. Roger Charman of Focus on the Family's Pastoral Ministries reports that approximately 20 percent of the calls received on their Pastoral Care Line are for help with issues such as pornography and compulsive sexual behavior. In a 2000 *Christianity Today* survey, 33 percent of clergy admitted to having visited a sexually explicit Web site. Statistics on Pornography, Sexual Addiction and Online Perpetrators, http://www.safefamilies.org/sfStats.php; compare Bissette, "Internet Pornography Statistics."

live a life of holiness that extends to our sexuality. Outside of marriage, we are unequivocally called to mental purity, verbal holiness, and sexual abstinence. There is no middle ground. As the apostle Paul states, "[We] are not [our] own; [we] were bought at a price." Therefore it is our mission and call to "honor God with [our] body" (1 Cor 6:19–20).

TWO

The Marital Challenge

WHAT MAKES FOR A long-lasting marriage? Is sexual fulfillment critical? Does marital mutuality play a role? And what about marriage itself? Is it God's best plan for us? The command to "Be fruitful and multiply" seems to exclude singleness (Gen 1:28). But can't someone serve God more fully, if he or she remains unmarried (1 Cor 7:32–34)? These are the questions that confront Christians living in a post-Christian society and the church ministering in a hypersexualized culture, where traditional biblical values have gone by the wayside.

THE PRACTICAL REALITIES

Today's society says sexual fulfillment is so critical for a good marriage that sexual experience is a must. Some go even further and say that living together before marriage is essential. We test-drive a car before we buy it, so why not do the same with a marriage partner? We try on clothes before we buy them, so why not a spouse? How else will a couple know if they are compatible for the long haul?

Far from ensuring a lasting marriage, studies actually reveal that relationships based primarily on sexual compatibility have a typical life span of three to seven years before failing.[1] In daily life, married couples spend less time in bed than they do in conversation, problem solving, and befriending one another. But when sexual compatibility dominates a relationship, the other key parts of the relationship suffer. Trust begins to erode, and control issues that require counseling often develop. These problems can be so severe that sexually active couples often do not make it to the altar.[2]

Also, sexual intimacy covers a multitude of faults and bumps in the road for newlyweds. Sex provides the marital "glue" during those early months of marriage.[3] Then sex takes its natural place beside the intellectual, emotional, and practical aspects of life. A couple that is sexually active before marriage has expended the marital resources intended for those first months of mutual exploration.

A premarital trial run has its pitfalls as well. Studies show that couples who live together are more likely to end up disagreeing rather than agreeing on key matters such as running a household, handling finances, and raising children.[4] Premarital counseling is where discussion of such matters should occur and where issues of marital compatibility are explored.

But what if two people really love each other? Isn't premarital sex a natural expression of their love? Although this is a common notion today, sexual intimacy early in a relationship is actually not sex at its best. To be sure, God created men and women with the capacity to give physical

---

1. Kaiser, "Questions on Dating & Sex," 45, 47–48.
2. Joy, *Bonding*, 56–68.
3. Kaiser, "Questions on Dating & Sex," 45, 47–48.
4. Joy, *Bonding*, 56–68.

pleasure to one another. But God intended this capacity to be the tie that binds a marriage. Sexual intimacy should be the gift we give our spouse on our wedding night: "I am my beloved's, and his desire is for me" (Song 7:10 NASB). God also intended sex to be the sign and seal of a lifelong commitment between two people: "Set me as a seal upon your heart, as a seal upon your arm; for love is strong as death, passion fierce as the grave. Its flashes are flashes of fire, a raging flame" (Song 8:6 NRSV).

What about gaining sexual experience before marriage? Doesn't this make someone a better partner when he or she does find the person with whom he or she wants to spend the rest of his or her life? The idea is that premarital sex develops the skills necessary to give pleasure to that special someone, when he or she comes along. Employers look for job experience. Wouldn't the same apply to marriage? Although this is also a popular notion, studies indicate that premarital sex actually puts a marriage at risk. It lays the basis for comparisons, doubts, and distrust. "Am I as good as his or her previous partner?" "If he didn't abstain before we got married, why would he be faithful now?" "Will she leave me, if someone better comes along?"[5]

Viewing sex as premarital practice also ignores the reality that sexual happiness grows only through years of intimate relationship. Sex is a skill. But it is a skill best learned in the context of marriage. The reality typically falls short of what is played on the big screen. Society teaches us to expect instant gratification, and the entertainment world projects instant success. A couple's first

---

5. See Fryling, "Why Wait for Sex?" 1.

experience typically falls short of the media hype and the standard romance novel. Good sex requires sensitivity to each other's needs and an interest in mutual satisfaction. It also requires trust, and trust is only built in the context of a lifelong commitment.

It is sometimes stated that, since the NT does not explicitly forbid premarital sex, it is one kind of sexual activity that is permissible. Arguments from silence should never be indulged in, however, especially apart from an understanding of the cultural context. The reason there is no explicit teaching on premarital sex is straightforward. Nearly all first-century girls, whether Jewish, Greek or Roman, married between the ages of twelve and sixteen. Puberty and matrimony occurred virtually at the same time. Moreover, the family line and its purity were of paramount importance. For this reason, virginity was a social necessity, and premarital sex was punishable by a court of law. Premarital sex defrauded a woman's future spouse of the physical intimacy that belonged to him.[6]

In the end, the intimacy that binds is sex between two people who have publicly vowed to commit to one another until death parts them. A lifelong commitment creates a context of safety and security for a man and a woman to freely give of themselves to one another. The exchange of public vows before friends and family provides accountability, and public vows before God and a local congregation add further accountability. The church not only witnesses but also commits to providing the support and resources to sustain and grow the marriage.

---

6. For an overview of marriage in the first century, see Belleville, *Women Leaders*, 71–96.

THE BIBLICAL REALITIES

What exactly does the Bible teach about marital intimacy? Jesus and Paul talk about the "two becoming one flesh" (Mark 10:7–8; Eph 5:32). But what exactly does this mean? The creation accounts of Gen 1–2 are the starting point for biblical answers, since what it means to be created "male and female" is fundamental to such questions:

> Then God said, "Let us make human beings in our image, in our likeness, so that they may rule over the fish in the sea and the birds in the sky, over the livestock and all the wild animals, and over all the creatures that move along the ground. So God created human beings in his own image, in the image of God he created them; male and female he created them. (Gen 1:26–27 TNIV)

> The man said, "This is now bone of my bones and flesh of my flesh; she shall be called 'woman,' for she was taken out of man." For this reason a man will leave his father and mother and be united to his wife, and they will become one flesh. (Gen 2:23–24)

Four basic truths about human sexuality as male and female can be gleaned from these texts. First, sexual distinction is divinely ordained. The creation of male and female was a calculated act on God's part: "Let us make" (1:26). It had as its goal the creation of two sexually distinct human beings: "God created human beings in our own image ... male and female he created them (TNIV)." While some translations have "God created *man*" and "he created *him*" (ESV, NASB, NASU, NKJV, NIV), this is not to suggest that God created an androgynous or bisexual human being. The Hebrew *ha 'adām* is a generic term for the human race—literally, "the earthling" or "earth-made"—hence the phrase, "Earth to earth, ashes to ashes, dust to dust."[7] Some put great emphasis on the English masculine "man" and "him" and attribute creation in God's image only to the male.[8] The Hebrew term, however, is not a proper noun or name for a masculine individual, Adam. The article *ha* with *'adām* makes this clear—God created "the human being." But what God created, he created as a twosome. He "created them male and female" and "he called them *'Adām*" (Gen 5:2).

The creation of a twosome is distinct from what precedes in the creative process. Unlike with the creation of the animals, a deliberative "Let us create" introduces this final step. The pomp and circumstance of the act is underlined by a shift to three parallel lines of poetry, which climax in the declaration: "Male and female he created them" (v. 27c). This is important. The creation of the human being as male and female is the very pinnacle of God's creative activity, the concluding fireworks display. To deny our sexuality, therefore, is to suppress our humanness. Even more, it is the sexual pairing of male and female that is the pinnacle of the creation process ("Let us make humankind in our image . . . male and female he created them"; vv. 26–27 NRSV). So to deny the distinction of the two sexes is to deny what was integral to God's final creative act. Jesus affirms this fundamental truth when he

---

7. Book of Common Prayer, "Burial of the Dead: Rite Two," 501.

8. See, for example, Ware, "Male and Female Complementarity," 20, who argues on the basis of this English translation that men bear God's image directly and women only derivatively; hence the priority of male over female.

states, "From the beginning of creation 'God made them male and female'" (Mark 10:6).

Second, intimacy is intrinsic to the male-female relationship. The divine intent is that "a man will be united to his wife, and they will become one flesh" (Gen 2:24). Both Jesus and Paul affirm this. Jesus states that the union of a man and a woman means "there are no longer two but one flesh" (Mark 10:8). Paul goes even further. The "two [male and female] will become one flesh" is nothing less than a type of the union of Christ and his church (Eph 5:31–32).

It then becomes important to understand what "two become one flesh" means. Sexual intimacy is certainly one aspect. Paul writes, "Do you not know that he who unites himself with a prostitute is one with her in body? For it is said, 'The two will become one flesh'" (1 Cor 6:16). Yet, in the thought-world of a Jew such as Paul, the term "flesh" (*bāsār*) meant much more than it does now. The Hebrew mindset viewed the whole person from different vantage points. It did not compartmentalize the human being into body, mind, and soul as Greek philosophers did.[9] "Flesh" viewed a person as mortal, "soul" is the self, "spirit" is a person viewed from the divine, immortal vantage point, and "heart" is viewing a person from the standpoint of the will or strength. For example, when Mary exclaims, "My soul magnifies the Lord," she means that she lifts the Lord up with her whole being, her entire self (Luke 1:46).

So, to speak of someone as "flesh" was another way of saying "mortal" or "human." Paul's use of the term exemplifies this meaning: "I declare to you, brothers and sisters, that flesh and blood cannot inherit the kingdom of God,

---

9. Westermann, *Genesis 1–11*, 233.

nor does the perishable inherit the imperishable" (1 Cor 15:50). Jesus said, "Blessed are you, Simon son of Jonah, for this was not revealed to you by flesh and blood, but by my Father in heaven" (Matt 17:17). Paul states, "For our struggle is not against flesh and blood, but against the rulers, against the authorities, against the powers of this dark world and against the spiritual forces of evil in the heavenly realms" (Eph 6:12). "Since the children have flesh and blood, he [Jesus] too shared in their humanity" (Heb 2:14). A union of "flesh" would then be a merging of two mortal human beings so that, in effect, where there were previously two, now there is only one.[10] This is God's perspective: "What God has joined together, let no one separate" (Matt 19:6). From a human perspective, "oneness" is not instantaneous. It starts at marriage and is ever progressing toward like-mindedness.

Third, the intended context for intimacy is a committed union. A man is to leave his parents and be united to his wife (Gen 2:24). He is to do so because the woman is, as Adam says, "bone of my bones and flesh of my flesh" (Gen 2:23). The language is thoroughly covenantal. In a Near-Eastern setting, bone-of-bones and flesh-of-flesh expresses not only kinship but also loyalty. It is an expression of loyalty similar to the marriage vow, "In sickness and in health . . . until death do us part."[11] That the phrase indicates a covenantal commitment is especially clear in

---

10. See, for example, Oswalt, "*Bāsār*," 136. In some places in the OT, the term "flesh" means "clan" or "kindred" (e.g., Lev 18:6; 25:49). Beeston, "One Flesh," 117; Skinner, *Genesis*, 70. Becoming "one flesh" would then mean becoming the equivalent of a blood relative, although this seems less likely in the context.

11. Book of Common Prayer.

Judges 9:2, where Abimelech uses the words, "I am your flesh and blood" to achieve an alliance with a people with whom he had no kinship bond.[12]

To form this union, "a man will leave his father and mother and be united to his wife" (Gen 2:24). The NIV translation "leave . . . and be united" is rather weak. The Hebrew word *'āzab* means "to forsake, abandon, desert."[13] Joshua commends the Reubenites, the Gadites, and the half-tribe of Manasseh because "to this very day" they "have not deserted the other Israelites but have carried out" their mission (Josh 22:3). An Egyptian slave states that his Amalekite master abandoned him when he became ill (1 Sam 30:13). The verb the NIV translates as "be united" is *dābaq*: "to cling, cleave to, hold fast."[14] Moses commands the people of Israel to "hold fast to the Lord [their] God and take [their] oaths in his name" (Deut 10:20; compare 11:22).

To "forsake" and to "cleave to" is covenantal language for the severing of one loyalty and the commencing of another.[15] In biblical times, the exclusive loyalty that a son showed to his parents was transferred to his wife. Because this was a society in which honoring parents was the highest obligation, this language speaks volumes about the biblical view of marriage as a bond requiring the strongest of

---

12. See Brueggemann, "Same Flesh and Bone," 532–42; Wilfong, "Genesis 2.18–24," 58–63.

13. BDB 738, a. *abandon*, (1) land, house, city, tent; a deserted region. b. *forsake*, (1) a man his parents, parent a child, wife her husband, an animal its young.

14. BDB 179, verb "to cling, cleave, keep close" a. fig. of loyalty, affection with the idea of physical proximity retained.

15. Hamilton, *Genesis*, 181; Wenham, *Genesis 1–15*, 71.

commitments and demanding an absolute and exclusive loyalty.

Fourth, masculinity and femininity are inherently good. "God saw all that he made" and that it was "very good" (Gen 1:31). To be male is good. To be female is good. Nowhere in Scripture are we encouraged to downplay sexual differences and move in a unisex direction. Our sports apparel and unisex clothing may do so today, but God does not intend that we follow this trend. Also, the sexuality that is deemed "very good" is male plus female. The union of male and female is lauded in Scripture from the creation accounts forward. Proverbs affirms the perpetual delight that a husband should find in the wife of his youth. She is "a loving doe" and "a graceful deer." Far from seeking greener pastures, the husband is to "ever be captivated by her love" (Prov 5:15–19). The Song of Solomon celebrates intimacy between a man and a woman: "I am my beloved's and my beloved is mine" (6:3 NRSV); "I am my beloved's, and his desire is for me" (7:10 NRSV). This intimacy, however, is set within the broader context of marital fidelity and a lifelong commitment. Virginity is intact before marriage. The bride-to-be is a "locked-up garden" and a "sealed fountain" (4:12). Vows are publicly exchanged. The wedding ceremony commences (4:1–15), the union is sealed (4:16—5:1), and the guests are invited to celebrate ("Eat . . . drink"; 5:1). The commitment is a lifelong one. The challenge to the groom is to place his bride "like a seal on [his] arm; for love is as strong as death . . . Many waters cannot quench love; rivers cannot wash it away" (8:6–7).[16]

---

16. The Song of Solomon can be plausibly understood as a commentary on Genesis 2:20–25. Davidson, "Theology of Sexuality," 1–19.

The same understanding of marriage is found in postexilic times: "The LORD was a witness between you and the wife of your youth ... she is your companion and your wife by covenant" (Mal 2:14). "A man leaves his own father, who brought him up, and his own country, and cleaves to his wife. With his wife he ends his days, with no thought of his father or his mother or his country" (1 Esd 4:20).

SEX, MARRIAGE & THE CHURCH

Noted ethicist Allen Verhey states, "Good sex is the embodied love of a man and a woman that expresses and sustains both intimacy and continuity and that signals a covenant undertaken in vows and carried out in fidelity."[17] Not all Christians are comfortable with such a sentiment. Prominent theologians throughout church history have claimed that sex is only to be engaged in for procreative purposes and that sex in any other context is sinful. Early church fathers such as Justin Martyr, Athenagoras, Clement of Alexandria, and Augustine matter-of-factly taught that sex in marriage should be undertaken only for the sake of reproduction. Other church fathers, who did not go this far, nonetheless counseled chaste moderation and even passionless sex.[18]

Some of the first-century Christians went even further and labeled sex itself as sinful. "Ascetic" is the theological term normally used for those who viewed sex (and like matters) in this way. For them the material world was

17. Verhey, "Holy Bible and Sanctified Sexuality," 41.

18. Justin Martyr, *Apology* 1:29; Athenagoras, *A Plea for the Christians*, 33; Clement of Alexandria, *Miscellanies*, 3.7.58; 12.70; Augustine, *On Marriage and Concupiscence*, 1.5.4; 1.17.15; Clark, "Sexuality," 843–44.

not morally indifferent (as the libertines thought), but downright evil. If one was to remain spiritually pure, contact with one's physical surroundings was to be avoided at all cost. Sex was physical; therefore, the body and its physical appetites were off-limits. This was the case even within the context of marriage.

An ascetic worldview was alive and well in the Corinthian congregation. Certain members claimed, "It is good for a man not to have sexual relations with a woman" (1 Cor 7:1 TNIV).[19] The phrase is literally "to touch a woman," and it is used both here and elsewhere as a euphemism for sexual intercourse.[20] This worldview can also be found in the Ephesian church. Paul states that there were those who were "forbidding people to marry and ordering them to abstain from certain foods" (1 Tim 4:3). Something similar was happening in the Colossian church. Their code of ethics included harsh treatment of the body and rules such as, "Do not handle! Do not taste! Do not touch!" (Col 2:20–23).

Paul himself, however, did not have an ascetic worldview. Some have misread the phrase "It is good for a man not to touch a woman" as Paul's opinion about how believers ought to deal with a society notorious for loose sexual morals and marital unfaithfulness. Recent translations such as the NRSV, REB, TNIV, and CEV have rightly put this text in quotation marks and understand it to be Paul's citation of a question the Corinthian church raised in a

---

19. Although some translate the Greek infinitive ἅπτεσθαι as "to marry," there is no lexical justification for this. LSJ ἅπτω 231; BDAG ἅπτω 126.

20. See, for example, Gen 20:6; Prov 6:29; Josephus, *Ant.* 1:163; Plutarch, *Moralia* 21.1.

recent letter to him ("Now concerning the matters about which you wrote"; 1 Cor 7:1a).

Not only is the ascetic point of view not Paul's view, but it also runs counter to what Paul and other biblical writers say elsewhere. The marriage union is something "created by God" and "good" (1 Tim 4:3–5). It is "an honorable estate" whose sexual integrity must be "respected by all" (Heb 13:4 NEB). The married couple is no longer "two" but "one flesh" (Gen 2:24; Matt 19:5; Mark 10:7–8; Eph 5:31). The husband and wife are not to sexually deprive each other except by mutual consent, and then only for a short time (1 Cor 7:5).

The biblical materials are uniform in teaching that sex plays a critical role in a lasting marriage. Paul, in particular, takes pains to spell out the sexual norms for the marriage relationship. They are noteworthy even by today's standards for what they say and do not say. For instance, they do not say that sex is for procreation. In fact, sex is not even connected with the propagation of the species. This is phenomenal, considering Judaism viewed the continuation of the family line of the utmost importance and the highest obligation.[21]

Also, Paul's sexual norms do not include anything about wifely submission. Nowhere does he say that a wife is to submit to her husband's sexual demands. This is amazing even by today's standards, where sex is still commonly viewed as the husband's privilege and the wife's obligation. First Corinthians 7 is especially striking for its total lack of patriarchy: "The husband should fulfill his duty" (v. 3); "the husband has no authority over his own body" (v. 4);

---

21. See, for example, Gen 38:8; Deut 25:5–6; Ruth 4:5.

"the husband must not divorce his wife" (vv. 11–12). These are remarkable norms given the male-dominated culture of the times.

The sexual norms Paul does affirm are equally surprising. First, the sexual needs of one's spouse are to be honored. Indeed, the meeting of those needs is considered the spouse's "due" (*tēn opheilēn*): "The husband should fulfill his marital duty to his wife, and likewise the wife to her husband" (1 Cor 7:3). The Greek is actually a command: "Let the husband fulfill . . . Let the wife fulfill." The Greek present tense indicates that meeting a spouse's sexual needs is an ongoing duty.

Second, intimacy is a matter of mutual consent. While sexual gratification is something "due" a spouse, it is not something that a spouse can insist on as a personal right. The husband has no authority to demand sex from his wife, and the wife has no authority to demand sex from her husband (1 Cor 7:4). In fact, the very opposite is true. "The marriage bed must be a place of mutuality—the husband seeking to satisfy his wife, the wife seeking to satisfy her husband. Marriage is not a place to 'stand up for your rights.' Marriage is a decision to serve the other, whether in bed or out" (1 Cor 7:4, *The Message*).

Third, sexual intimacy is to be expressed between one man and one woman. Neither polygamy nor same-sex marriage was a cultural option in the first century. Nor are they biblical options. Paul's description of marriage is explicit: "Each man should have his own wife, and each woman her own husband" (1 Cor 7:2). The divine plan is one man and one woman. The "two" (not three, four, or more) become "one." And it is a man and a woman (not

The Marital Challenge

male plus male or female plus female) that are to "cleave" to one another (Gen 2:24 NASB).[22]

Fourth, there is no place for lust in the marriage relationship. Paul has blunt words for those who view marriage primarily as a sexual escape valve. Each man is to learn how to live with his wife "in holiness and honor and not with lustful passion like the pagans who do not know God" (1 Thess 4:4–5 NLT).[23]

Fifth, sexual intimacy is central to the marriage relationship. The two becoming one flesh is not just a figure of speech. Each partner belongs to the other so fully that Paul can call the withholding of physical intimacy an unlawful deprivation: "Stop depriving one another, except by agreement for a time, so that you may devote yourselves to prayer, and come together again so that Satan will not tempt you because of your lack of self-control" (1 Cor 7:5 NASB).[24] Exceptions require mutual consent.

---

22. See chapter 3 for further treatment.

23. Interpretations of *skeuos* in 1 Thess 4:4 are divided. A *skeuos* is literally an earthen vessel or clay pot. Figuratively, *skeuos* refers to what is mortal or fragile. In the context of this passage, *skeuos* as one's mortal body or as the weaker, more fragile gender are the main options. Both find a place in the NT. Paul refers to the treasure of the gospel housed in the *skeuos*, or earthen vessel, of the gospel preacher (2 Cor 4:7). Peter speaks of the wife as the "weaker," that is, the more fragile, *skeuos* (1 Pet 3:7). The infinitive *ktasthai* means "to get, to acquire" (L&N §57.58), which fits better with *skeuos* as "wife" than as "one's body." "Acquiring a wife" was a first-century practice in which marriages were contracted between families and involved financial pledges and dowries. If *skeuos* means "one's body," then 1 Thess 4:4 would refer to treating (literally "keeping") one's body in a holy and honorable fashion.

24. The Greek word *apostereite* means to deprive someone of something that is rightfully and legally theirs. Compare 1 Tim 6:5, "deprived of the truth" (NASB). L&N §57.47.

The theme throughout 1 Cor 7 is mutuality. Paul insists on absolute reciprocity in the marriage relationship; there is no ground that the husband or wife can claim as his or her own. Each sexual norm is carefully and precisely balanced: "Each man should" and "each woman should" (1 Cor 7:2); "the husband must" and "the wife must" (v. 3); "the wife's body does not" and "the husband's body does not." Mutuality extends even to the matter of initiating (or not initiating) a divorce. A wife must not divorce her husband, and a husband must not divorce his wife (vv. 10–11). A husband must not divorce his unbelieving wife, and a wife must not divorce her unbelieving husband (vv. 12–13).

Paul's statements are quite countercultural for his time. The Roman world of the NT was strikingly similar to our own. Roman women were becoming less interested in having children, and the average number of children per household was about 1.75. The divorce rate was comparable to today's, and the most commonly filed lawsuits were for alimony and child support.[25] Sexual mutuality and marital commitment were qualities lacking in Paul's society and of similar ministerial concern for the church.

THE DIVINE PLAN FOR SINGLES

The command to be fruitful and multiply (Gen 1:28) and the intent for male and female to become "one flesh" (Gen 2:24) raise the question of whether there is a place in the divine plan for the single person. To be single and sexu-

---

25. The emperor was so concerned about the lack of males to serve in the Roman armies that he made marriage a requirement for women. Belleville, *Women Leaders*, 90–96.

ally active is certainly not a biblical option. But there is definitely a place in the biblical scheme for the celibate single.

The creation command "Be fruitful and multiply" comes before the command to "rule over" creation (Gen 1:28). The ability of humans to exercise dominion over creation depends on the propagation of the species. The sequence of ideas in Genesis 1 shows that creation in God's image is what enables humankind to be caretakers of what God has created: "Let us make the 'adām in our image" comes first. "And let them have dominion" over all the earth comes second (Gen 1:26–30 NRSV).

At what point does the human race become sufficiently fruitful to carry out the task of dominion over creation? And when does the command "Be fruitful and multiply" no longer apply? The population of human beings was certainly sufficient by the time of Abraham: "These are the clans of Noah's sons ... From these [clans], the nations spread out over all the earth after the flood" (Gen 10:32—11:1). In fact, the command to be fruitful and multiply is not found after the postflood expansion. Instead we find God turning to the task of creating a people who desired worship and fellowship. The goal was to develop one nation that could be "a light to all the nations" (Gen 12:1–3; 15:1–18; 17:1–7; 22:16–18). Abraham and his descendants were that nation.

Abraham's descendants become the people of Israel, who dedicated themselves to loving God with all their heart, mind, and strength (Deut 6:5). Their mission was to bear witness that Abraham's God was the only true divine being and that the many gods and goddesses of the surrounding nations were fabricated out of ignorance:

"Hear O Israel: the LORD our God, the LORD is one" (Deut 6:4; compare Acts 17:22–31). As such, Israel's God alone is deserving of worship (Deut 6:1). Israel's mission also included preserving the purity of the family line, clan, tribe, and nation. To this end, marriages were contracted between families, adulthood celebrated at age twelve, and marriages consummated shortly thereafter. God's people were forbidden to marry outside Israel (Deut 7:3–4). Mosaic law provided for the lack of a son to carry on the family name. If a man died before producing a son, it became the responsibility of the nearest in-law to provide a son for the deceased with the deceased man's wife ("kinsman-redeemer"; Deut 25:5–10).

With the advent of the church in NT times and salvation through faith in Christ, marriage and progeny were no longer a priority. One looks in vain in the NT for a command to be fruitful and multiply. Instead, singleness is lifted up as having the advantage over marriage. Both have intrinsic worth and significance, but singleness frees the believer to be wholly focused on ministry and kingdom service. Jesus calls attention to "those who have renounced marriage because of the kingdom of heaven" (Matt 19:12). "Not everyone can accept this [singleness]," he states (v. 11). But God provides for all the needs of those who can (vv. 11–12). In short, Jesus recognizes an alternative path to marriage where there is a commitment to advance the work of God's kingdom. But he is realistic about this path. Those who choose it cannot go it alone; they need God's enablement ("to whom it has been given"; v. 11).

It is surely Jesus' teaching on this subject (rather than mere personal predisposition) that leads Paul to tell the Corinthian church that marriage is good but singleness is better. In response to a question about the superiority of the single life to the married life, Paul acknowledges that on general principle it is good to remain unmarried (1 Cor 7: 8). This applies to widows and widowers (vv. 8, 40), to those pledged to be married (vv. 26, 38), and to the unmarried in general (v. 27). Paul is also quick to add, as Jesus does, that this path requires divinely enabled "self-control" (vv. 2, 5, 9).

The rationale Paul gives for the superiority of the single life is twofold. First, those who marry face many troubles in this life (v. 28).[26] Paul is probably thinking about the agonizing decisions family responsibilities force on a person, especially in times of crisis (v. 26). "Those who marry will face many troubles in this life, and I want to spare you this," he says (v. 28). Second, an unmarried person is free to give undivided attention to kingdom matters. "The time is short ... For this world in its present form is passing away" (vv. 29–31). Therefore, the work of ministry is urgent. "An unmarried [person] is concerned about the Lord's affairs—how he can please the Lord" (v. 32). The key phrase is "the Lord's affairs." Singleness affords more time and therefore more opportunity for serving God.

Some think Paul would not have advocated singleness if he hadn't believed that Christ's return was just around the corner. Paul's language of "the present crisis" (v. 26) and "the time is short" (v. 29) is suggestive. But it ignores the immediate context. The interests of those who are married are divided; the interests of those who are single are not (vv. 32–35). This is an ageless truth. Also, the Greek does not require the translation "the present crisis."

---

26. Literally, "persecution because of the flesh" (*thlipsin tē sarki*).

It can equally be rendered "life's pressing needs" or "the present obligations" (*tēn enestōsan anankēn*). Life is short; therefore, time is of the essence in terms of spreading the good news of Jesus Christ.

This is not to say that getting married or fulfilling one's marital and family responsibilities is wrong. Early in 1 Cor 7, Paul calls devotion to the needs of one's spouse a marital "obligation" (v. 3). Elsewhere, he commands the husband to "love his wife as he loves himself" (Eph 5:33) and to "bring up" his children "in the training and instruction of the Lord" (Eph 6:4). But all this takes time. For this reason, the married person has "divided interests," while the single person does not (1 Cor 7:34). Nor is Paul saying that marriage is not good. He states unambiguously that the marriage union is something "created by God" and "good" (1 Tim 4:3–5). Yet, for the sake of the gospel ministry, the single life has its advantages. So we would be remiss as a church if we did not encourage gifted people to follow this path of service.

There is no double standard. God calls men and women alike to remain unmarried for the sake of the gospel. Just as a married man "is concerned about the affairs of this world—how he can please his wife—and his interests are divided" (1 Cor 7:33), so too a married woman "is concerned about the affairs of this world—how she can please her husband" (v. 34). And just as "an unmarried man" can be fully "concerned about the Lord's affairs" (v. 32), so also "an unmarried woman" can be fully "concerned about the Lord's affairs" (v. 34). The bottom line for both is that they "live in a right way in undivided devotion to the Lord" (v. 35).

The superiority of singleness for full devotion to kingdom service explains Paul's statement in Gal 3:28 that in Christ "there is no longer male and female" (NLT, NRSV). The other pairings are correlated: "neither Jew nor Gentile" (*ouk . . . oude*), "neither slave nor free" (*ouk . . . oude*). The third pairing, however, is negated as a unit: "not male and female" (*ouk . . . kai*). Paul's language recalls the creation narratives: "God created human beings in his image, in the image of God he created them, *male and female he created them*" (Gen 1:27 NLT; compare NRSV, NET). The female was created as a "help" (KJV; not "helper," NIV) or "partner" (NRSV; *ēzer*). She was created because God deemed, "It is not good that the man should be alone" (Gen 2:18). So God created someone said to be "meet for" or "corresponding to" (*kᵉnegdō*) the male. To accomplish this, the woman was created "out of" (*ek*) the man and "for his sake" (*dia ton andra*; 1 Cor 11:8–9).

"In the Lord, however," the status quo of male and female changes (1 Cor 11:11). In creation, "male and female" become "one flesh" (Gen 2:24); in the church, male and female function as individuals and not as a unit or single entity. They are no longer "male–and–female" (Gal 3:28) Yet, men per se and women per se are not totally independent of one another. "Woman is not independent of man or man independent of woman," states Paul (v. 11). Although there is no longer marital oneness (married couples functioning as a "unit"), there is gender interdependence (individuals partnering in worship and service). Paul notes in 1 Cor 11:4–5 that men prayed and prophesied alongside women who prayed and prophesied. There were not two worship services, one for the women and another for the men. Also, each person (not married couples) brought his or her respective gifts to the worship service. Paul states, "When you come together, everyone has a hymn, or a word of instruction, a revelation, a tongue or an interpretation" (1 Cor 14:26). The key is that "all of these must be done for the strengthening of the church" (v. 26) and "in a fitting and orderly way" (v. 40).

Paul's analogy is that of the human body with its individual members cooperating and interdependent: "The body is a unit, though it is made up of many parts; and though all its parts are many, they form one body. So it is with Christ" (1 Cor 12:11–12). *Each* has a gift. *Each* contributes to the work of ministry (Eph 4:12 NRSV). The unity does not come from the oneness of marriage but "the work of one and the same Spirit" who "gives [gifts] to each one, just as he determines" (1 Cor 12:10). In terms of ministry and service, singleness has its definite advantages. As Jesus noted, the harvest is plentiful but the workers are few (Luke 10:2).

The bottom line, however, is that whether single or married, male or female, Jew or Gentile, slave or free, we are called as Christians to a life of holiness that extends to our sexuality. Outside marriage, we are unequivocally called to sexual abstinence. There is no compromising on this one. Inside marriage, we are called to a relationship of mutual consent, mutual respect, and regarding matters of sexual intimacy, a forsaking of all thoughts and actions that put the marital "oneness" at risk. If our ministry and service are to be fruitful, sexual integrity is a must.

THREE

The Same-Sex Challenge

SAME-SEX ISSUES ARE SOME of the most daunting that Christians face today. In part, this is because gay activists have been implementing a finely tuned agenda over the last four decades about which the general public remains largely in the dark. An extensive network of resources and organizations attests to their accomplishments. Politically, they have their activist associations, legal organizations, financial resources, insurance groups, and highly trained lobbyists.[1] Educationally, there are the periodic gay-awareness events, a historical society and museum, a highly influential teachers' caucus, school youth clubs, young adult empowerment groups, and a parent organization.[2] Clergy support includes an association and

1. The Gay and Lesbian Activists Alliance (GLAA) was founded in 1971. The Lambda Legal Defense and Education Fund was established in 1973. The Gay & Lesbian Alliance Against Defamation (GLAAD) has been in place since 1985. GaySurance.com is dedicated to providing members of the LGBT Community with assistance in obtaining insurance for any number of needs.

2. Gay, Lesbian, Independent School Teachers Network (since 1985; now the Gay, Lesbian, and Straight Teachers Network or GLSTN) and the Gay, Lesbian and Straight Education Network (GLSEN, since 1990) are two of the most powerful and effective gay networks. The Gay, Lesbian, Bisexual Transgender Historical Society (GLBTHS, since 1985) is located in San Francisco. Virtually every urban high school

scholarly journals.[3] Social networking happens through widely circulating magazines, ads, television and movie networks, and a search engine with over eight thousand links.[4] There are also urban websites that include gender-specific accommodations, restaurants, bars, gyms, health clubs, hair salons, health-care professionals, tax services, and churches.[5]

Lesbian activists have made significant strides of late. Several precedent-setting cases have been successfully litigated and two key projects launched "to ensure a brighter future" for all gay and lesbian young people in schools, at home, in foster care, in the juvenile justice system, and in sports.[6] The public image of lesbians has

---

and university now has a Gay-Straight Alliance (GSA) group on campus (since 1998). There are also gay-pride days, days of silence / nights of noise, and synergy dances. Young adult groups include the Lesbian, Gay, Bisexual, Transgender & Questioning Youth (LGBTQ) and Youth Empowerment Alliance (YEA). Parents, Families and Friends of Lesbians and Gays (PFLAG) is also very active.

3. See *Clergy United for the Equality of Homosexuals (CUEH)*; *Bridges: A Journal for Jewish Feminists and Our Friends*; the *Gay Theological Journal*.

4. See, for example, the annual Pride parades commemorating the 1969 New York City Stonewall riots and the gay Olympic games (hosted by Chicago in 2007). Magazines include *Advocate*, *Planet Out*, *Whosoever*, *Anything That Moves*, and *Alternative Family*. Ads can be placed in *The Commercial Closet* (since 1995). TV networks include *Frameline* (since 1976) and *Dyke TV* (now in reruns). *Brokeback Mountain*, *Fire*, *Philadelphia*, and *Milk* have been lauded as first-rate movies.

5. Popular search engines include BluWay, Inc. (www.bluway.com); www.sistertrip.com; www.qguys.com.

6. The National Center for Lesbian Rights (NCLR) litigates precedent-setting cases at the trial and appellate court levels, conducts community seminars, and advocates for equitable public policies. *Youth*

changed. Lesbianism has become "cool." A recent survey of 1.35 million preteen and teenage readers of *CosmoGirl!* indicates that 60 percent have a friend who is lesbian or bisexual.[7] Experimentation in high school and college has become an in-thing. Subscriptions to lesbian magazines are on the rise. Internet websites are seemingly endless, providing information and resources for such matters as adoption, civil unions, custody, visitation rights, donor insemination, family law, parenting, and schools.[8]

Same-sex marriage promises to be one of the biggest challenges of the twenty-first century. It has been an issue in every political campaign since the early 1990s. Residents in virtually every state have faced ballot initiatives or legislation for and against it. Demonstrations in the name of "civil rights" have become a familiar sight. And rallies in favor of same-sex marriage are widespread.

Same-sex marriages have become a particular dilemma for the church. Hardly a month goes by where the same-sex issue does not surface as a newsworthy item in some quarter. Most mainline denominations have had to

---

Project was started in 1993 and *SportsProject* in 2001. http://www.nclrights.org.

7. Yndigoyen, "*CosmoGirl!* Includes Queer Peers."

8. See hrc.org. *Lesbian News* has a global readership of over 120,000. *In the Family* and *Baby* factor in same-sex parents and adopted children. *Curve* profiles interesting lesbian women. *Go* claims to be the cultural roadmap for the city lesbian. *Lesbian Travel* highlights lesbian vacation hot spots, and *Lesbian Archives* has the coming-out stories of older "sisters." There is *Lesbian Love Advice* for problems with your girlfriend. *Lesbian Movies & Lesbian Theatre* reviews the latest lesbian films, plays, and documentary studies. *Lesbianbooks.com* provides the latest lesbian novels and book reviews. *Lesbianhotspots.com* has the latest lesbian entertainment and music festivals. *Lesbiancalendar.com* has upcoming lesbian events, workshops, activities, and meetings.

deal annually with overtures regarding the ordination of homosexuals and the acceptance of same-sex marriages. Majority and minority reports abound.[9]

Evangelicals have not avoided the limelight. In 1986, the Evangelical Women's Caucus International voted in support of its lesbian minority.[10] Nationwide associations like Evangelicals Concerned, Soulforce, and Other Sheep have become a familiar part of the evangelical landscape, and "sexual minorities" and "civil rights for oppressed peoples" have become common catchphrases. Youth have been a distinct focus. In spring of 2006, Soulforce created a youth arm, whose stated mission is to provide support for college-age gays and to expose "oppressive, non-affirming homosexual policies" of known Christian colleges and universities.[11] An evangelical, gay denomination, the Universal

---

9. See, for example, recent headlines and statements about United Methodist (UM), Reformed Church in America (RCA), Presbyterian (PC-USA), Evangelical Lutheran (ELCA), and Episcopal churches: "RCA Minister Who Presided at Gay Daughter's Wedding Defrocked" (2009); "United Methodist Court Rejects Gay Marriage Resolution" (2009); "Episcopal Church Splits over Gay Equality" (December 2008); "PCUSA June 2008 Assembly Approves Deleting Gay Clergy Ban"; via Cumberlink.com;"ELCA August 2007 Assembly Approves Homosexual Lutheran Clergy Who Are in Sexual Relationships to Serve as Pastors." Soulforce demonstrated at the United Methodist 2008 General Conference April 25–27 in Fort Worth, Texas, requiring a conference delay of several hours.

10. *Update: Newsletter of the Evangelical Women's Caucus*, 6.

11. In spring 2006, a bus of about seventeen young adults visited Abilene, Azusa Pacific, Bethel, Biola, California Baptist, Colorado Christian, Eastern, Lee, North Central, Oklahoma Baptist, Oral Roberts, Regent, Union, and Wheaton. In spring 2007, one bus went to Dordt, Oklahoma Baptist, Baylor, Mississippi, Union, Covenant, Montreat, Messiah, Gordon, Cedarville, Cornerstone, and Calvin, while another bus went to MidAmerica North, Fresno Pacific, George

Fellowship of Metropolitan Community Churches (MCC), claims a membership of about 50,000. MCC churches can be found in virtually every urban area.[12]

Interest in same-sex issues is relatively new. Up until recently, the Western world uniformly condemned sexual intimacy with someone of the same gender. As early as Roman imperial times, sexual activity between persons of the same sex was a capital offense. The church down through the centuries regarded such intimacy as forbidden. Ecclesial authorities without exception considered same-sex relations to be a violation of God's law.[13]

A shift in perception occurred in the 1950s, when the social sciences began attributing same-sex attraction to environmental conditioning—one parent being close-

---

Fox, Seattle Pacific, Northwest, and Northwest Nazarene. In fall 2008, Liberty, Columbia, Morehouse, Spelman, Palm Beach Atlantic, Heritage Christian, Mississippi, Louisiana, Dallas Baptist, Southwestern Baptist Theological Seminary, Southwestern Assemblies of God, Ouachita Baptist Central Baptist, Union, and Simmons were visited. http://www.soulforce.org/article/1431.

12. Evangelicals Concerned was founded in 1971 by psychotherapist Ralph Blair (www.evangelicalsconcerned.org). Other Sheep was founded in 1992 by OT scholar and missionary Tom Hanks (www.othersheep.org). Soulforce was founded in 1999 by Metropolitan Community Church pastor Mel White and his partner Gary Nixon (www.soulforce.org). The first worship service of the MCC was held in the greater Los Angeles area in 1968. The MCC claims to have about three hundred congregations in twenty-two countries. The MCC is affiliated with the Lesbian Gay Bisexual Transgender association (LGBT; www.mccchurch.org).

13. See, for example, Polycarp, *To the Philippians* 5.1 (2nd century); Hippolytus, *Refutation of All Heresies* 5.2.18 (3rd century); Eusebius, *Demonstration of the Gospel* 4.10.6 (4th century); Chrysostom, *Homily on Titus* 5 (5th century). For further treatment, see Wright, "Homosexuality," 435–36.

binding and overprotective, the other being hostile and/or distant. Such findings led the British Parliament in 1967 to decriminalize same-sex relations between consenting adults over the age of twenty-one.[14] In 1973, the American Psychiatric Association (APA) followed suit and removed homosexuality from the *Diagnostic and Statistical Manual of Mental Disorders*.[15] The APA removed homosexuality from its *DSM* list in response to activist lobbying and demonstrations. The decision was not based on any advance in scientific or medical knowledge. In fact, the executive board of the APA had to ignore considerable psychological data that showed homosexuality was a reversible disorder. Significantly, the members of the APA who specialized in treating homosexuals protested the board's decision.[16]

Currently, it is not uncommon to have homosexuality presented as a normal alternative, akin to left-handedness. Any form of counseling or attempt to change the sexual orientation of a client is now deemed by the American Psychological Association as "unethical."[17]

14. Freeman, *Sexual Offences Act*

15. *Diagnostic and Statistical Manual*, 532.

16. For a treatment and evaluation of the issues, see Martin and Martin, "Developmental and Ethical Issues," 58–68; Satinover, *Homosexuality and Politics*; Nicolosi, *Reparative Therapy*; Moberly, *New Christian Ethic*.

17. In 1997, the American Psychological Association (APA) passed a resolution expressing concern that clients may request conversion therapy due to "societal ignorance and prejudice about same-gender sexual orientation" and "family or social coercion and/or lack of information." In March 1998, the American Counseling Association (ACA) passed a similar resolution at its annual convention. Since most states automatically adopt subsequent revisions of the ACA code of ethics, mental health counselors who propose change as an option are in danger of review by state licensing authorities. In August 2009, the APA

The impact of the APA's actions on American society has been profound. In 1960, all fifty states had laws banning same-sex relationships. Today, these laws have been repealed in all but three states, and even these have been deemed unconstitutional by the U.S. Supreme Court.[18] Civil ceremonies with marriage-like vows between same-sex couples who register with the city as domestic partners have become routine in most urban areas. What constitutes a marital union has become so questionable that the U.S. Census Bureau announced in 2000 that it would no longer be collecting data on marriage and related matters.[19] That the term "marriage" is in flux is evident in the Merriam-Webster Dictionary's addition in 2003 of the secondary meaning, "the state of being united to a person of the same sex in a relationship like that of a traditional marriage."[20]

Such changes have not gone unnoticed by American voters. Same-sex relationships have been a politically divisive issue. On May 28, 1996, Congress passed the Defense of Marriage Act, defining marriage as "a union of one man and one woman."[21] Yet, in December of that same year, a circuit court ruling in Hawaii voided a state marriage

---

rejected gay-to-straight therapy outright by a vote of 125 to 4. Crary, "Gay-To-Straight Therapy," A2.

18. *Lawrence v. Texas*, March 26, 2003.

19. U.S. Census Bureau, "Marriage and Divorce Data."

20. *Merriam-Webster's Collegiate Dictionary*, 11th ed., s.v. "Marriage."

21. United States Code, "Definition of 'Marriage' and 'Spouse,'" 1.1.7: "In determining the meaning of any Act of Congress, or of any ruling, regulation, or interpretation of the various administrative bureaus and agencies of the United States, the word 'marriage' means only a legal union between one man and one woman as husband and wife, and the word 'spouse' refers only to a person of the opposite sex who is a husband or a wife."

license prohibition for same-sex couples. So, while the federal government does not recognize same-sex marriages, recognition at the state level is another matter. By 2010, same-sex marriages were legal in Massachusetts, Connecticut, New Hampshire, Vermont, and Iowa. Maine also legalized same-sex marriages in May 2009, but the decision was repealed by popular vote six months later.[22] Other states are scrambling to put legislation in place that would refuse recognition of same-sex marriages performed in other states.[23] All are grappling with the legal and moral implications.

Changing attitudes about same-sex relations are due in part to the sexual climate in the United States. Sex is looked on as a constitutionally protected right. It is believed that we have a right to fulfill our biological drives in whatever manner we see fit, a right to any sexual course of action we desire, and a right to privacy. Effective strategies have done the rest. LGBT has targeted three strategic venues: public policy, education, and the media.

In 1996, the National Gay and Lesbian Task Force Policy Institute produced a blueprint for the second Clinton administration regarding gay and lesbian issues. Implementation began in 1998, when the president issued an executive order giving preferential treatment to the

---

22. Massachusetts governor Mitt Romney ordered town clerks to begin issuing marriage licenses on May 17, 2004. Connecticut followed suit four years later, and then Iowa, Vermont, and New Hampshire in 2009. Abel, "Same-Sex Marriage Bills," 1.

23. Proposition 8, defining marriage as between a man and a woman, was passed by the voters of California in the November 2009 elections. Its constitutionality was challenged August 2010 by a United States District Court judge.

hiring of gays in the civil service sector, starting with the White House.[24]

The next step was a revamping of the public school curriculum. The National Educators Association (NEA) mandated one month per year of sensitivity education in all federally funded schools. The goal was to encourage youth to explore homosexuality as a "healthy," "normal," and "viable" sexual identity.[25] In 1997, the nation's school curriculum was revamped to include a homosexual component. *It's Elementary: Talking about Gay Issues in School* is now shown in public schools throughout the United States from kindergarten through sixth grade. Homosexuality is presented as "kind of like vegetables: You don't know [you'll like it] until you try."[26] In 2000, the NEA developed a primer for principals, educators, and school personnel, *Just the Facts About Sexual Orientation & Youth*, which attempts to discredit therapy that offers hope for change by claiming that it only promotes increased self-hatred, harassment, and violence.[27] The Education Network has now

24. Associated Press, "House Kills Bid," 6.

25. See, for example, the establishment of the *Journal of Gay and Lesbian Issues in Education* (Hawthorn Press, 1996).

26. Other films include *Choosing Children* (1984), a documentary about lesbians becoming parents; *That's a Family!* (2000), a video that aims to help elementary school-age children see and understand the many different shapes that families take today; and *One Wedding and a Revolution* (2004), a behind-the-scenes look at the days leading up to San Francisco Mayor Gavin Newsom's decision to allow lesbian and gay couples to marry. These can be found on http://www.womedia.org.

27. Ex-gay reparative groups such as Exodus International and Courage are said to be a front for right-wing political efforts to promote an ultra-conservative, sectarian agenda that aims to destroy the important wall of separation between church and state. This publica-

posted a twenty-day school lesson plan titled "What's With The Dress, Jack?" that encourages, among other things, cross-dressing and non-gender-conforming clothing.[28]

The results of such curricular changes are noteworthy. A decade ago, high school and college gay-support groups were virtually nonexistent. Today, it is the rare urban and suburban school that does not have multiple groups.[29] Teacher-staffed support groups, gay pride rallies, days of silence, book and magazine displays, bulletin boards, hallway posters, newsletters, faculty institutes, field trips, gay dances, and gay proms have become a familiar part of the high-school environment. The college and university scene is a virtual replica. To date, the educators' network has created more than 4000 nationwide school clubs.[30]

The impact of LGBT strategies on the media is also noteworthy. Ten years ago, homosexuals were not scripted

---

tion can be found on www.apa.org/pi/lgbc/facts.pdf; www.outfront.org/library/fact.html; and www.glsen.org.

28. This curriculum can be obtained from the Gay, Lesbian and Straight Education Network of Los Angeles and found on www.glsenla.org.

29. Besides GSA, other names of GLSEN-sponsored groups include *Spirit Club*; *Pride*; PRISM; *Students Understand Diverse Sexualities* (SUDS); *Students Promoting Unity & Diversity* (SPUDS); *Accepting Sexual Orientation in Schools* (As.Is); *Lesbian, Gay, Bisexual, Transgender Ally Alliance* (LGBTA); *Straight & Gay Alliance* (SAGA); *Gay & Straight Student–Faculty Alliance* (GSSFA); *Diversity Club*; *Trust Club*; *Committed To Action* (CTA); *Place For All* (PFA); and *Gay, Lesbian And Straight Students* (GLASS). To check gay and lesbian clubs at a particular high school, one can go to http://en.wikipedia.org/wiki/Bartlett_High_School,_Bartlett,_Illinois and substitute the high school's name, city, and state.

30. See the Gay, Lesbian, and Straight Education Network Library on http://www.glsen.org and www.campuspride.net.

into television series. Today, it is the rare television series that does not cast for gay and lesbian parts and treat the theme as normal. Ellen Degeneres's 1996 decision to "come out" was formative in the creation of high-profile lesbian characters, including an orthopedic surgeon on *Grey's Anatomy*, a publicist on *Melrose Place*, a town mayor on *Friday Night Lights*, an anesthesiologist on *Nip/Tuck*, and Gretchen on *Heroes*. High-profile gays characters include a bartender on *Grey's Anatomy*, a nurse on *Mercy*, an accountant on *The Office*, a paramedic on *Trauma*, a police officer on *Southland*, and a student on *Glee*.

THE SCIENTIFIC CHALLENGES

"Everyone knows homosexuality is genetic and change is impossible." "You are born gay and can't do anything about it, so accept the fact that you are and move on." These and similar statements are all too common today. But are they factual? Part of the difficulty is that we do not receive balanced reporting on the topic. For example, on July 15, 1993, the National Public Radio reported the discovery of the gene that causes homosexuality. The next day's headline in the *Wall Street Journal* read, "Research Points Toward a Gay Gene," and a *New York Times* headline read, "Report Suggests Homosexuality Is Linked to Genes." This byline was based on a seven-page article in the journal of *Science* entitled, "A Linkage between DNA Markers on the X-Chromosome and Male Sexual Orientation."[31] However, four months later in the same journal, genetics researchers from Yale, Columbia, and Louisiana State Universities took issue with the assumptions and statistics

31. Hamer, "Linkage between DNA Markers," 321–27.

that underlie the article's conclusions. At the same time, a review of 135 research studies appeared in the *Archives of General Psychiatry*, concluding that there was no evidence to substantiate a biological theory of homosexuality. The primary factor was deemed to be environmental conditioning: a close-binding, overprotective mother and a distant, nonaffirming father.[32] Yet, this information did not make it into the hands of the general public.

A wide range of other studies has been put forward as supporting a biological basis for homosexuality. There have been reports of a relationship between homosexuality and chromosome abnormality;[33] the size of the hypothalamus;[34] the size of the spleen;[35] hormone levels;[36] finger length;[37] left-handedness, dyslexia, and stuttering;[38] and twin studies,[39] giving the cumulative impression that

---

32. Risch et al., "Male Sexual Orientation," 2063–65; Byne and Parsons, "Human Sexual Orientation," 228–39.

33. Turner, "Homosexuality, Type 1," 109–34.

34. LeVay, "Difference in Hypothalamic Structure," 1034–37; Swaab et al., "Gender and Sexual Orientation," 51–61.

35. De Lacoste-Utamsing and Holloway, "Sexual Dimorphism," 1431–32. Replica studies failed to substantiate.

36. Bahlburg, "Sex Hormones and Male Homosexuality," 297–325; Adkins-Regan, "Sex Hormones and Sexual Orientation, 335–47; Feder, "Hormones and Sexual Behavior," 165–200; McCormick and Wittlesons, "Cognitive Profile," 459–73; Ehrhardt and Meyer-Bahlburg, "Effects of prenatal sex hormones," 1312–18.

37. Williams et al., "Finger-Length Ratios," 455–56.

38. See, for example, Lindesay, "Laterality Shift," 965–69; McCormick et al., "Left-handedness," 69–76; Gotestam et al., "Handedness, Dyslexia and Twinning," 179–86; Lalumière et al., "Sexual Orientation," 575–92.

39. See, for instance, Kallmann, "Comparative Twin Study," 137–59; J. Michael Bailey and Pillard, "Genetic Study," 1089–96; J. Michael Bailey et al., "Heritable Factors," 217–23; Whitam et al., "Homosexual Orientation," 187–206.

The Same-Sex Challenge

homosexuality is genetically hardwired and therefore immutable. Yet each study has failed to replicate its findings. The claimed linkage between DNA markers on the X-chromosome and homosexual orientation is one of those. D. H. Hamer and his research team retracted their conclusions two years later because of the inability to corroborate the original report.[40]

In some cases, further studies have not only failed to corroborate the original reports but actually produced opposite findings. For example, further hormone studies showed no link between hormonal levels and homosexuality and concluded that sexual orientation and hormone treatment are unsuccessful in influencing sexual orientation.[41] A 1992 identical-twins study is another example. Although the media claimed a roughly 50 percent concordance as proof-positive, the researchers themselves concluded that the genetic factors were insufficient to explain the development of sexual orientation. For one, the sample was small (forty-six identical twins); and two, the concordance was in reality significantly low. The fact that the twins shared not only genes but also prenatal and familial environments should have resulted in a percentage much higher than 50 percent. More, further studies of

---

40. Hamer et al., "Linkage between Sexual Orientation," 248–56. Crewdson, "Study Challenged," A10–11.

41. See the substantive critiques by Stanton Jones and Yarhouse, "Science and the Ecclesiastical Debates," 446–77; Byne and Parsons, "Human Sexual Orientation," 228; Whitehead, "Science and Homosexuality"; the National Association for Research and Therapy of Homosexuality (www.NARTH.com).

twins raised apart supported nurture and environment as the factors, rather than a shared genetic code.[42]

THE PSYCHOLOGICAL CHALLENGES

"I don't ever remember a time when I wasn't attracted to the same sex, so my same-sex feelings must be inborn." Such recollections have been deemed definitive confirmation that homosexuality is innate. What is overlooked, however, is that socialization begins at birth and recollections don't go back that far. There is also ample evidence that gender identity is established by the age of three and is largely in response to social factors such as nurture and child-rearing practices.[43] The earliest years of life are those when the brain rapidly develops and gender identity forms. So what appears as innate—"nature," is actually an early-learned experience—"nurture."

Psychotherapists with the National Association for Research and Therapy of Homosexuality (NARTH) have found several common social threads in the experiences of gays and lesbians. One thread is a disruption during the toddler years of the childhood need for love from, dependency on, and identification with the same-sex parent for boys, or for approval from their father or other male adult figure for girls. This disruption can take the form of physical absence, emotional remoteness, or personal disapproval.[44] Because sexual-identity formation develops during the early years, a father who travels can

42. King and McDonald, "Homosexuals Who are Twins," 407–9; Eckert et al., "Monozygotic Twins," 421–25.

43. Green, *Sissy Boy Syndrome*.

44. Moberly, *New Christian Ethic*, 1–16.

The Same-Sex Challenge

be perceived by a sensitive child as abandonment: "He leaves because of me."[45]

Another common thread in the experiences of gays and lesbians is the resistance on the part of the child to reattach to a parent in spite of the parent's best efforts. The sexual growth process comes to a halt. Girls stop playing dress-up as mommy and boys as daddy. The child becomes "stuck" in the gender-developmental cycle. The need, then, is to repair the disrupted relationship. Sexual development typically resumes once a parental or surrogate-parental attachment is successfully achieved.[46]

What NARTH therapists suggest is that same-sex attraction is not the problem per se but rather a *symptom* of unresolved issues. The underlying problem is the absence of formation through same-sex identification during early childhood. Same-sex attraction can thus be seen as the result of the unfulfilled childhood need for parental love and approval—whether perceived or real. Same-sex relationships then become an adult's unknowing attempt to fulfill that childhood need. Affirmation received from an older gay man or lesbian woman is often the entry point into the gay-lesbian community and corresponding lifestyle.[47]

The psychological and emotional dysfunction underlying same-sex attraction makes committed relationships difficult. For this reason, same-sex unions aren't typically monogamous, and faithfulness is not of a traditional sort. A recent survey of 156 stable, committed male couples of

---

45. Worthen and Davies, *Someone I Love Is Gay*, 114–36; Nicolosi and Nicolosi, *Parent's Guide*, 19–63.

46. See, for example, Nicolosi, *Reparative Therapy*, 25–76.

47. See the concise overview in Moberly, *New Christian Ethic*, 1–16 and Nicolosi and Nicolosi, *Parent's Guide*, 147–81.

five or more years' duration reported that 62 percent had had sexual encounters during the year prior to the survey, and that the average number of extra-relational partners was 7.1. "Monogamy" is consequently not a word the religious gay community uses. Instead, fidelity is characterized as living in "a loving, caring, honest relationship with your partner."[48]

Perceived nonaffirmation is typically what leads same-sex partners to split up, whatever the length of the relationship. Gay and lesbian relationships often become a broken record, replaying the defensive detachment from the perceived unrequited parental love experienced during childhood. The perceived or real absence of parental love not only brings confusion and insecurity but also leaves an emotional wound or "scar" in the psyche. Some people go on to spend their entire adult lives attempting to fill the vacuum created by unrequited parental love.[49]

This is not to discount the complexities of same-sex attraction. Nature and nurture are acknowledged pieces of the puzzle. But it is important to distinguish between predisposition as a contributing factor and a homosexual orientation gene. Boys possessing an artistic temperament and talent (nature) are often labeled as "sissies" and excluded by the other boys. Girls possessing athletic ability are often labeled as "tomboys" and excluded by the other girls. It is for this reason that psychologists typically refer

---

48. Stanton Jones and Yarhouse, *Homosexuality: The Use of Scientific Research*, 24.

49. Lindenfield, *Emotional Healing*, 3–18.

to homosexuality as a complex interaction between talents, temperament, and environment.[50]

Indeed, clinicians such as Robert Spitzer, who played a key role in the APA's 1973 decision to deem homosexuality as inborn and hence untreatable, are now conceding the key role that a person's social environment plays and have found that treatment has been effective in a significant number of cases.[51] Warren Throckmorton, past president of the American Mental Health Counselors Association, and Christopher Rosik, a prominent marriage and family therapist, report that modifications of a homosexual orientation have been effective and should be available to clients requesting such assistance.[52] Gay neurobiologist Simon LeVay and notable psychologist Douglas Haldeman have publicly acknowledged that therapy should be an option.[53] Northwestern University psychology professor, J. Michael Bailey, calls same-sex attraction "evolutionarily maladaptive" in his 2003 volume *The Man Who Would Be Queen: The Science of Gender-Bending and Transsexualism*.[54]

---

50. Stanton Jones and Yarhouse, *Homosexuality: The Use of Scientific Research*, 18.

51. Spitzer, "Can Gay Men and Lesbians Change Orientation?" 403–17.

52. Throckmorton, "Attempts to Modify," 283–304; Rosik, "When Therapists," 39–45.

53. Haldeman, "Gays, Ex-Gays, Ex-Ex-Gays"; Simon LeVay, "Sexual Orientation," forthcoming.

54. J. Michael Bailey, *Man Who Would Be Queen*, 116. Bailey's work was deemed politically incorrect and he was asked to step down as department chair at Northwestern University. Bailey stirred up controversy two years later as senior author of a study that claimed that male bisexuality does not exist. Carey, "Straight, Gay, or Lying?"

THE EVANGELICAL CHALLENGES

Some evangelicals have recently argued that to believe in the mutuality of men and women (commonly called "egalitarianism") is to be on a slippery slope to lesbianism or on the way to a gay-affirming stance. Some go so far as to name names and lay blame: "Few egalitarians have yet to advocate the moral validity of homosexual conduct but it is just a matter of time."[55] A telltale sign of being on the path to liberalism is allowing women to teach Bible. And if an organization is not already on the path to liberalism, a telltale sign of movement in that direction is the use of gender-neutral Bibles like the TNIV and the NRSV.[56]

Such statements and conclusions betray a fundamental ignorance of the psychology of same-sex attraction and the testimonies of gay and lesbian strugglers themselves. Without understanding the origin of the desires, mere behavioral attempts to control the drive create a lifetime of frustration and guilt.[57] This is particularly the case with lesbianism. What therapists and strugglers alike have found to be common to the experiences of lesbians is a pattern of male victimization typically found in hi-

---

55. See, for example, David Jones, "Egalitarianism and Homosexuality," 12–13; Grudem, *Evangelical Feminism*, 3, 237–39. Grudem claims that places where evangelical feminism already has much influence are Bethel Seminary, Dallas Seminary, Denver Seminary, Concordia Seminary, Asbury Seminary, Gordon-Conwell Theological Seminary, Reformed Theological Seminary Orlando, Wheaton College, Azusa Pacific University, Regent College, InterVarsity Press, Baker Academic Books, *Christianity Today*, InterVarsity Christian Fellowship, the Baptist General Conference, the Vineyard, and the Willow Creek Association.

56. See Grudem, *Evangelical Feminism*, 3, 237–39.

57. Moberly, *New Christian Ethic*, 20–21.

The Same-Sex Challenge

erarchical settings with strong role differentiation. Male victimization is the foremost shaping factor for the vast majority of lesbians who seek therapy. It is the father (or other male family member) who sexually and/or emotionally abuses his daughter, or it is the dad who does the same to the mom. Deep fear and even hatred of men develops. Intimacy and affirmation are sought within the perceived safety of a same-sex context.[58]

Some evangelicals go even further and claim that non-hierarchical families (those which operate by mutual consent and mutual submission) end up with a dad who is a wimp, a mom who is a usurper, children who lack discipline and respect for authority, unmasculine and unattractive guys, unfeminine and unattractive gals, and spouses who are ambivalent about sex. A family that operates by male leadership and female submission, on the other hand, has a strong dad, a gentle mom, well-behaved and authority-respecting children, masculine guys, feminine gals, and sex that is mutually fulfilling.[59]

Yet the scenario that commonly leads a female to embrace lesbianism is not an ineffectual father and usurping mother, but just the opposite. It is typically that of a weak, ineffective mom who is under the thumb of a controlling husband. Daughters pick up many clues about being "feminine" by observing their father's (or other male authority figure's) attitude toward their mother. If the attitude is negative, then being feminine can easily be perceived as "unsafe" or "weak," a conclusion often reinforced by male sexual exploitation during the girl's teenage years.

---

58. Nicolosi and Nicolosi, *Parent's Guide*, 147–65.
59. Grudem, "Key Issues," 70–73.

A woman's deep need to connect with another individual draws her into close relationship with other women who have been wounded in the same way. This then sets the stage for lesbian bonds to occur.[60]

Restoration works in reverse to the way in which the original wounding occurred. The "cure" is very much like that for alcoholics, who have low self-esteem and a lifetime of unhealthy living habits.[61] It is not a matter of just "stopping" or remaining celibate. As with most types of psychological and emotional change, the growth process is long and arduous. One of the first tasks of recovery is to de-emphasize sexual identity and emphasize one's true identity as a son or daughter of God. At the same time, there is the need for strong, loving relationships that affirm the worth and significance of the struggler as a human being created in God's image and thus deserving of respect and support.[62]

For most gays and lesbians, transformation is a lengthy process. For some, it takes years of therapy devoted to rebuilding self-esteem and sexual identity. John Paulk states, "I was able to forgive my parents for their emotional neglect and the way I felt they had rejected me. The lack of forgiveness that held me captive for so long began melting away."[63] The support of Christian community that extends unconditional love and forgiveness, when mistakes are made, is critical. For some this support takes the form of godly, strong women who challenge the belief that to be

---

60. Worthen and Davies, *Someone I Love Is Gay*, 82, 129.
61. Moberly, *New Christian Ethic*, 20–21.
62. Worthen and Davies, *Someone I Love Is Gay*, 82, 129.
63. Paulk, *Not Afraid To Change*, 191–204.

feminine is to be weak. For others, the key is being in a community with men who treat women with dignity and equality, which frees them to embrace their gender and to feel safe as a woman.[64] For still others, the turning point is contact with a church that has a vision and a will to reach out to gays and lesbians.[65]

A critical factor for those struggling with sexual identity issues is developing healthy same-sex friendships. Support groups led by leaders who have experienced change is central to the healing process. Therapy that focuses on the root causes and issues of homosexuality is also important. As repair and healing occur, the common experience of gays and lesbians is that attractions for the same sex diminish and attractions for the opposite sex increase. In short, the process of sexual development from same-sex identification to opposite-sex attraction, which stalled in the early years, is now able to move forward. In the end, the single most important component is the will to continue over the long haul. All agree that the path to sexual wholeness is not for the faint of heart or for those looking for a quick fix.[66]

THE BIBLICAL CHALLENGES

What about the Bible? Is there room in Scripture for something other than a heterosexual lifestyle?[67] Religious gays answer in the affirmative. Biblical passages explicitly pro-

---

64. Sneeringer, "Safe as a Woman."

65. Tracy, "Cornered By Grace."

66. See "Real Stories" at http://exodus.to/content/view/417/180.

67. The most substantial treatment to date is Gagnon, *Bible and Homosexual Practice*.

hibiting same-sex relations are said to be a mere handful and therefore unimportant. "The Bible is an empty closet," states Ralph Blair, the director of Evangelicals Concerned. "It has nothing to say against same-sex relations but everything to say about God's grace and love."[68] A 1993 pamphlet by Other Sheep's founder, Tom Hanks, identifies homosexuality as the "fifth" spiritual law: It is "a gift of God to be embraced, celebrated, and lived out with integrity."[69]

That the explicit prohibitions are few in number is true. There are two prohibitions in the OT and three in the NT. What is also true, however, is that they are unequivocal in their rejection of same-sex pairings: "Do not lie with a man as one lies with a woman" (Lev 18:22); "If a man lies with a man as one lies with a woman, both of them have done what is detestable" (Lev 20:13); "Even their women exchanged natural relations for unnatural ones. In the same way the men also abandoned natural relations with women and were inflamed with lust for one another. Men committed indecent acts with other men" (Rom 1:26–27); "Do not be deceived! Neither male prostitutes nor men who have sex with men will inherit the kingdom of God" (1 Cor 6:9–10 AT). "The law is for the law-defying . . . men who have sex with men (1 Tim 1:10 AT).

At the same time, the pairing of male and female is lifted up without exception as the rule throughout biblical times and beyond.[70] Humankind as "male and female" is by divine design: "So God created human beings in his own image. In the image of God he created them; male

68. Blair, "Bible is an Empty Closet."

69. Steve Parelli is the current director of Other Sheep; compare Parelli, "Homosexuality and the Bible."

70. Wright, "Homosexuality," 435–36.

and female he created them" (Gen 1:27 NLT). Divine design includes distinction. God created a "masculine" (*zakar*) as distinct from a "feminine" (*neqēbah*) human being.[71] Divine design also includes similarity. The female was created from the male's breastbone, making her "bone of [his] bones" and "flesh of [his] flesh" (Gen 2:23). The divine intent was to make a union of the two: "they will become one flesh" (Gen 2:24). It is with this end in view that the male is "to leave his father and mother" and "cleave to" the female (v. 24 NASB). The NT reaffirms this intent. Jesus states, "They are no longer two but one (Mark 10:8); it is "God" who "joined them together" and only God who "can separate them" (Matt 19:6; Mark 10:6). Paul goes even further, calling the union of male and female an image of the union of Christ and the church (Eph 5:32).

Equally important is the fact that God's people throughout history unanimously rejected same-sex unions as unnatural and affirmed heterosexual pairings as natural. "And why do not the Eleans and Thebans," asked Jewish historian Josephus, "abolish that unnatural and impudent lust, which makes them lie with males?" (*Ag. Ap.* 2.273).[72] "Our laws own no other mixture of the sexes but that which nature has appointed of a man with his wife" (2.199). The moralistic *Sibylline Oracles* states, "Men must not share their bed with other men" (2.73).[73] Same-sex prohibitions

---

71. The Hebrew *zakar* (LXX *arsen*) and *neqēbah* (LXX *thēly*) are distinctly "masculine" and "feminine," respectively. BDB 271 and TWOT 551.

72. Elea (or Elis) and Thebes were regions of the province of Achaia. "Unnatural" translates the Greek phrase *para physin*, literally "against nature."

73. See also *Sib. Or.* 3.185; 3.764; 5.166–67.

based on "nature" are identical to those of the biblical texts. Sodom's sin was men discarding "the law of nature" (Philo, *Abr.* 135–36). Not only the sexual pairing of males with males but also females with females is "against nature" (Pseudo-Phocylides, *Sententiae* 192).

The church fathers also uniformly rejected same-sex relationships as unnatural and indecent, while affirming opposite-sex ones as natural and seemly. Polycarp states, "It is a good thing to refrain from lusts in the world ... neither male prostitutes nor men who defile themselves with men shall inherit the kingdom of God" (*To the Philippians* 5.1).[74] Hippolytus speaks of men who, "leaving the natural use of the woman, burned in their lust one toward another; men with men working that which is unseemly" (*Refutation of All Heresies* 5.2.18).[75] Eusebius commands his readers, "Do not defile yourselves with any of these things," such as "the union of women with women and men with men" (*Demonstration of the Gospel* 4.10.6). John Chrysostom exclaims, "O you subverter of all decency, who use men, as if they were women" (*Homily on Titus* 5).

The Old Testament Prohibitions

> "Do not lie with a man as one lies with a woman (*meta arsenos ou koimēthēsē koitēn gynaikos*); that is detestable." (Lev 18:22)

> "If a man lies with a man as one lies with a woman (*hos an koimēthē meta arsenos koitēn gynaikos*), both of them have done what is detestable. They

---

74. See also Aristides, *Apology* 9.8–9; Theophilus, *Ad Autolycum* 1.2, 14.

75. Compare Origen, *Against Celsus* 7.49.

The Same-Sex Challenge

must be put to death; their blood will be on their own heads." (Lev 20:13)

Some say that the OT same-sex prohibitions are located in passages dealing with obsolete physical impurities, and that the laws found in Leviticus are tied to a religious system that is no longer in effect. "Do not give any of your children to be sacrificed to Molech" (Lev 18:21; 20:1–5) has to do with antiquated Canaanite religious practices, and "Do not approach a woman to have sexual relations during the uncleanness of her monthly period" (Lev 18:19; 20:18) is an archaic taboo. So "Do not lie with a man as one lies with a woman" (Lev 18:22; 20:13) must then be equally obsolete. Jesus himself, it is claimed, made this clear. When the Pharisees accused him and his disciples of breaking the Law by eating without first performing the ceremonial hand washing, Jesus said, "Nothing that enters one from outside can defile that person" (Mark 7:15 NAB). Such laws are thus no longer valid.[76]

What is overlooked, however, is the fact that all the sexual practices prohibited in Lev 18 and 20, with the exception of child sacrifice, bestiality, and menstrual intimacy, are also prohibited in the NT. This is especially the case with capital offenses such as incest, adultery, and same-sex practices. Sexual intimacy with a family member or relative is similarly condemned by the Apostle Paul: "It is actually reported that a man has his father's wife" (1 Cor 5:1–10).[77] Adultery is denounced by one and all.[78] And a

76. See, for example, Thurston, "Leviticus 18:22," 7–23.

77. Compare Lev 18:6–18; 20:11–12, 17–21.

78. Matt 5:27–28; 15:19; 19:16; Mark 7:20; Rom 13:9; 1 Cor 6:9; Heb 13:4; 2 Pet 2:14; Rev 2:22.

sexual relationship between men is forbidden: "Do not be deceived! Neither the sexually immoral (*pornoi*) . . . nor men-who-bed-men (*arsenokoitai*) . . . will inherit the kingdom of God" (1 Cor 6:9–10).

Nor is it a matter of Mosaic laws being set aside by gospel grace. For the OT same-sex prohibitions are declared to be contrary to law and gospel alike.[79] The action of "men who have sex with men (*arsenokoitai*)," says the Apostle Paul, "is contrary to the sound doctrine that conforms to the glorious gospel" (1 Tim 1:10–11), and "in the gospel a righteousness from God is revealed . . . so that those who do such things deserve death" (Rom 1:17–32). This makes same-sex activity a universal moral wrong and not a temporary cultural or religious taboo.

It is true that prohibitions against child sacrifice and menstrual intimacy are not repeated in the NT. The Levitical "Do not give any of your children to be sacrificed to Molech" (18:21) and "Do not approach a woman to have sexual relations during the uncleanness of her monthly period" (18:19) are not reiterated in the NT. But neither is the prohibition against bestiality: "Do not have sexual relations with an animal and defile yourself with it" (Lev 18:23; cf. Exod 22:19; Deut 27:21). Yet, there is virtual consensus regarding the moral wrongness of bestiality.[80] In antiquity, Aristotle is representative: Bestiality is "evidence that what distinguishes human from animal is entirely lacking in those who do it" (*Nicomachean Ethics* 7.1150a1). Today, bestiality (clinically known as zoophil-

---

79. Compare Lev 18:22; 20:13.

80. Bestiality is similarly condemned in Exod 22:19, "Anyone who has sexual relations with an animal must be put to death" and Deut 27:21, "Cursed is the man who has sexual relations with any animal."

The Same-Sex Challenge

ia), or sexual attraction to and relationships with animals, is classified as a DSM IV pathology.[81]

The absence of child sacrifice, menstrual intimacy, and bestiality prohibitions in the NT can be readily explained. All three were Canaanite practices, not first-century Greco-Roman ones. Leviticus 18:27 makes this connection quite plain: "All these things were done by the people who lived in the land before you." The influence of indigenous peoples has been confirmed by archeological findings.[82] Hittite law approved of homosexual acts unless they were incestuous or against one's will.[83] Although Assyrian law called for the castration of any male imposing himself on another male, consensual relationships seem to have been another matter (*Middle Assyrian Laws* 19–20). The same appears to have been the case in Mesopotamian culture.[84]

The OT language of *clean* and *unclean* is typically pointed to as indicative of archaic restrictions. Thurston, for example, maintains that Lev 18 and 20 have to do with ritual cleanliness rather than sexual morality and hence do not apply today.[85] What is not said, however, is that the same language appears in the NT. The Apostle Paul states

81. *Diagnostic and Statistical Manual*, 532.

82. Wenham, "Old Testament Attitude," 359–63.

83. Lev 18:22–27; 20:13–15. See "Middle Eastern Religious Practices and Institutions," *Encyclopaedia Britannica*, 15th ed. Ugaritic texts shed no light on corresponding Canaanite attitudes. Wenham, "Old Testament Attitude," 359–63.

84. Wenham states that it is clear from iconographic evidence dating from 3000 BC to the Christian era that homosexual practice was an accepted part of the Mesopotamian scene ("Homosexualität," 559–68).

85. Thurston, "Leviticus 18:22," 7–23.

that believers have been *washed* and *cleansed* of sexually immoral acts such as "men having sex with other men" (1 Cor 6:9–11). The author of Hebrews commands that the marriage bed be kept *undefiled* (Heb 13:4). *Clean*, *washed*, and *undefiled* have a spiritual dimension through the indwelling work of the *Holy* Spirit and thus cannot be dismissed or written off as outdated.[86] "Do you not know," Paul states, "that your body is a temple of the Holy Spirit, who is in you, whom you have received from God? You are not your own; you were bought at a price. Therefore honor God with your body" (1 Cor 6:19–20).

It is critical to note that the prohibitions of Lev 18:22 and 20:13 go beyond an ethic of personal purity to reinforce the sexual boundaries of the created order of male and female. God created the human being in his own image as male and female (Gen 1:24). Thus, a male (*arsen*) is not to have sexual intercourse with another male (*meta arsenos ou*). And to do so is deserving of death (Lev 18:22; 20:13).

Some think that these passages have in view something other than an adult consensual relationship, such as pedophilia, rape, or prostitution. However, the Hebrew "male" (*zakar*) rather than "youth" (*na'ar*) excludes pedophilia and boy prostitutes. The equal punishment of the parties involved indicates that both are consenting adults. "Their blood will be on their own heads" (Lev 20:13) shows that both are aware of what they are doing and of the consequences.

---

86. For further discussion, see Lane, *Hebrews 9–13*, 516–17.

Sodom and Gibeah

Genesis 19 (Sodom) and Judg 19 (Gibeah) are a testimony to the fact that Israel had to be concerned about local sexual practices:

> The men of the city, the men of Sodom, both young and old, all the people to the last man, surrounded the house; and they called to Lot, "Where are the men who came to you tonight? Bring them out to us, so that we may know them." (Gen 19:4–5 NRSV)

> The men of the city . . . surrounded the house, beating on the door. And they said to the old man, the master of the house, "Bring out the man who came into your house, that we may know him." (Judg 19:22 ESV)

Some claim that Sodom and Gibeah's sin was not that of sexual immorality, but rather an indifference toward those who needed food and shelter. Ezekiel 16:49 is typically invoked as the interpretive key, "Now this was the sin of your sister Sodom: She and her daughters were arrogant, overfed and unconcerned; they did not help the poor and needy." It is argued that Ezek 16:49 shows that the issue was the flouting of Middle-Eastern hospitality obligations toward the traveler and not sexual impropriety. When "all the men from every part of the city of Sodom, both young and old, surrounded the house" and demanded, "bring [the visitors] out to us so that we may *know* them" (Gen 19:4–5; Judg 19:22), they were not seeking sex but demanding to see their credentials. Just as security guards check a person's bona fides at a border crossing, so the men of Sodom were wanting "to know" the visitors' reasons for being in Sodom and Gibeah.[87]

The context, however, makes it clear that the demands of the Sodomites and Benjamites were sexual in nature. For one thing, the verb "to know" (*yada'*) is recognized by Hebrew lexicographers as a standard euphemism for sexual intercourse.[88] Adam "*knew* (*yada'*) his wife Eve, and she conceived and bore Cain" (Gen 4:1). Abishag the Shunammite "became the king's attendant and served him, but the king *did not know her* [*lo' y^{e}da'ah*]" (1 Kgs 1:3–4). Similarly Lot's daughter had "*not known* a man" (Gen 19:8), and the Benjamites "*knew* and abused" the Levite's mistress "all night long" (Judg 19:25).

But is same-sex activity even an issue here?[89] Perhaps the intent had been to abuse the male visitors in the sense of slapping them around during an interrogation, which only turned sexual when women became involved. Again, the specifics of the biblical texts seem clear, and the Judeo-Christian tradition uniformly identifies the intent as homosexual. Josephus states, "When the Sodomites saw the young men to be of beautiful countenances, and this to an extraordinary degree, and that they took up their lodgings with Lot, they resolved themselves to enjoy these beautiful boys by force and violence" (*Ant.* 1.200–201). Jude 7 says that the Sodomites "gave themselves up utterly" not only to "sexual immorality" but also to "going after strange

---

87. Sherwin Bailey, *Western Christian Tradition*, 4–5.

88. Harrison, "Know," 3:48; Westermann, *Genesis 12–36*, 301; Gerstenberger, "ידע," 1051–55.

89. Scholars are right to point out that these texts technically have to do with gang rape. But that the activity included men sexually desiring other men is inescapable.

flesh," an idiom for engaging in anal intercourse.[90] Second Peter 2:7–10 speaks of "those who indulged their flesh in depraved lust." Philo interprets the activity as "men who discarded the law of nature . . . and lusted after one another" (*Abr.* 133–36). Church historians agree. Methodius states that "wine and strong drink" goaded the inhabitants of Sodom "to an unnatural and fruitless desire for males" (*Banquet* 5.5). Regarding their sexual organs, Augustine states, "the Sodomites were steeped in sin" (*On Marriage and Concupiscence* 2.34), and John Chrysostom speaks of the depravity of men seeking men and women seeking women (*Homily 4 on Romans*).

What then is one to make of Ezek 16:49? What do Sodom and same-sex relations have to do with the sin of "pride, excess of food, and prosperous ease"? First, the overall context makes it clear that aping the idolatrous practices of the Canaanites is the fundamental sin. Ezekiel's indictment of Jerusalem is that she went beyond her "younger sister, Sodom and her daughters," for she not only "walked in their ways and copied their detestable practices" but also poured out her wealth and exposed her nakedness in her promiscuity with her lovers—all her detestable idols, and gave them her children's blood" (Ezek 16:36, 46–47, 50, 57–58). This is also how Philo understood it. In his estimation it was "overmuch prosperity" and the inability "to bear [it] discreetly" that led the Sodomites to "discard the laws of nature" and engage in deviant sexual activity (*Abr.* 133–35).

---

90. L&N §88.279 ἀπέρχομαι ὀπίσω σαρκὸς ἑτέρας literally "to go after strange flesh"; to have homosexual intercourse: "They committed homosexual intercourse . . . like the people of Sodom and Gomorrah" (Jude 7).

Jesus' Teaching & Greek Practices

There are three passages in the NT that explicitly deal with same-sex practices. All three are in Paul's writings. None are found in the teaching of Jesus. Is this because Jesus did not consider same-sex relations to be a big deal? Some have said so.[91] But Jesus' silence is readily explained. The specific sexual practices that he targeted were those that were a reality in the Jewish circles in which he moved. The challenges of Jewish culture included adultery (Matt 5:32; 19:9; Mark 7:22; 10:11–12; Luke 16:18; 18:20; cf. John 7:53—8:11), prostitution (Luke 15:30), children born out of wedlock (John 8:41), and divorce (Matt 5:31–32; 19:1–12; Mark 10:1–12). Same-gendered sex, however, was not a practice of the Jews of that day. So it is hardly surprising that it does not surface as an issue in Jesus' teaching.

If Jesus had addressed same-sex activity, in all probability the standard would have been equal to or higher than that of Mosaic law. His specific pronouncements about other sexual matters certainly demand a higher standard. "Do not commit adultery" (Exod 20:14; Deut 5:18) becomes "anyone who looks at a woman lustfully has already committed adultery with her in his heart" (Matt 5:27–28). "Anyone who divorces his wife . . . is not allowed to marry her again" (Deut 24:1–4) becomes "anyone who divorces his wife except for marital unfaithfulness causes her to commit adultery" (Matt 5:31–32).

That the topic of homosexuality appears in Paul's writings is equally easy to explain. He was, after all, apostle to the Gentiles, the very cultural context in which same-

---

91. See, for example, Sherwin Bailey, *Western Christian Tradition*, 4–5.

The Same-Sex Challenge

sex relationships surfaced. Unlike the broad-based, cross-class activity today, same-sex relationships in antiquity were largely confined to the upper crust of Greek society. Also unlike today, it was "an honorable service" for a young Greek male student to be intimate with his male mentor.[92] Plato recounts, "In our city [Athens] both [the mentor] loving someone and showing affection to one's lover [the student] are held in highest honor" (*Banquet* 183–85). The first-century Greek historian Plutarch confirms the practice: "When the boys reached the age of 12, they were favored with the society of lovers from among the reputable young men. The elderly men also kept close watch of them" (*Lycurgus* 17–18).[93]

The same can be said of all-girl schools. Plutarch remarks that "boy lovers ... were so approved among them [the Spartans] that even young girls found lovers in good and noble women" (*Lycurgus* 18.9). The most well-known was Lesbos, the home of the ancient Greek lyric poet Sappho and site of the all-girls school that she ran. Her poems exhibit strong feelings of affection and passion for

---

92. Such intimacy did not extend to anal intercourse, which Greeks considered to lower person to the level of a beast. Sexual fondling and intercrural stimulation were the extent of the practice. Such fondling is captured on Greek vases of the period. Belleville, "Facts and Fictions," 65–86.

93. What was not sanctioned was male prostitution. It was considered a reprehensible degradation of the Greek ideal that love between men cannot be bought or sold. See, for example, Plato, *Banquet* 184B. See also Cantarella, *Pandora's Daughters*, 77–89.

her students.[94] Whether they were sexual or platonic is an ongoing matter of debate.[95]

Beyond puberty, however, sexual intimacy between men was deemed "against nature." Plato states, "If we were to follow in nature's steps and enact that law which held good before the days of Laius [King of Thebes], we would declare that it is right to refrain from indulging in the same kind of intimacy with men and boys as with women, and offer as evidence the nature of wild beasts, pointing out how male does not touch male for this purpose, since it is *unnatural*" (Plato, *Laws* 836c).[96]

Even so, some young men had difficulty ending the relationship. The declaration of love made by Alcibiades as a young man and student of Socrates is a case in point:

---

94. Most of her poems are preserved only in the quotations of other authors. See, for example, Plutarch, *Dialogue on Love* 751: "Sappho addressed a young girl not yet ripe for marriage: 'You seemed to me a small child without favor.'"

95. The extent of lesbian relationships in Greek society is difficult to determine. Communities of women did exist (for example, on the island of Lesbos). And it is speculated that sexual encounters were part of the educational process for young females in these communal settings. But there is a lack of hardcore evidence. Nonpederastic sexual activity between women is mentioned but only in a handful of Greek and Roman sources. All but Plato (who treats it in theory) postdate Paul. See Plato, *Banquet* 189D–191E; Lucian, *Affairs of the Heart* 28; Martial, *Epigram* 1.90; 7.67, 70.

96. This differs from the early Plato, who understood humanity as originally created as three sexual beings: male, female, and hermaphroditic (a "man-woman"). As a punishment for conspiring against the gods, each hermaphrodite was split in half so that its attentions might forever be focused on seeking unity with its "better half" (Plato, *Banquet* 189–92).

> I went and met him, and the two of us would be alone; and I thought he would seize the chance of talking to me as a lover (*erastēs*) does to his dear one (*erōmenos*) in private, and I was glad. But nothing of the sort occurred at all. He would merely converse with me in his usual manner... Then, as I made no progress that way, I resolved to charge full tilt at the man... Accordingly I invited him to dine with me, for all the world like a lover scheming to ensnare his darling. (Plato, *Banquet* 217)

Affection and intimacies also developed between men thrown together for an extended period of time. The fourth-century BC veteran mercenary Xenophon wrote, "Thebians and the Eleans shared common beds... and assigned places to their favorites alongside themselves in the battle-line" (*Banquet* 8:32, 37). Such a practice was not confined to the Greek military. As late as the AD ninth century, it was noted by Roman Emperor Basil and his troops that the defeated Arab military included "men who share their beds with men" (Greek Anthology *Epigram* 9.686). Emperor Justinian in the sixth century amended the Julian Law Code to include practicing homosexuals, with death as the penalty (*Institutes* 4, 18, 2–3 *Corpus Iurus Civilis*).

Intimate relationships likewise developed in communities of women in high society circles, the goddess cults, and female guilds. Explicit references are scarce during the Hellenistic period. Whether this is due to a lack of female authors or the rarity of such activity is difficult to determine. Yet, the first-century Jew Pseudo-Phocylides not only mentions but also forbids it, showing that some form of it existed in the NT period: "Let women not imitate the sexual role of men" (*Sententiae* 192). Most Greek and Roman moralists target Philaenis of Samos, a high-class Greek mistress who authored a manual on the techniques of seduction, sexual positions, aphrodisiacs, abortion drugs, cosmetics, and the like (*P. Oxy.* 29 §2891). The first-century Roman satirist Martial says, "You, Philaenis, lesbian to women who also are lesbians, rightly call her whom you *poke* a girlfriend . . . you cudgel eleven girls every day" (*Epigram* 1.90; 7.67, 70). Mid-second-century Greek rhetorician and satirist Lucian states, "Let wanton lesbianism—that word seldom heard which I feel ashamed even to utter—freely parade itself, and let our women's chamber emulate Philaenis, disgracing themselves with Sapphic amours" (*Affairs of the Heart* 28).

First-century moralists uniformly rejected same-sex activity, whether male-male or female-female pairings. Jewish moralist Pseudo-Phocylides commanded his male readers to "not commit adultery nor rouse homosexual passion" (3–5) and his female readers to "not imitate the sexual role of men" (192). The post first-century *Sibylline Oracles* similarly told its readers, "Men must not have sex with men (*Mē arsenokoitein*)" (2.73).[97] Greek moralist and historian Plutarch called males consorting with males "a completely ill-favored, indecent, an unlovely affront to Aphrodite" (*Dialogue On Love* 751D–752B). Romans viewed male-male sexual activity as a practice of barbarians.[98] Although 149 BC Roman *Lex Scantinia* is only

97. Compare *Sib. Or.* 3.185; 3.764; 5.166–67.

98. Although Emperor Nero's fetish for young men is sometimes cited as typical Roman practice, there is every indication that Romans disapproved of such activity. Also, the factuality of such a fetish has

extant in the quotations of later authors, there is every indication that it legislated the death penalty for same-sex behavior.[99]

Plato's words sum up what became the prevailing Hellenistic viewpoint: "When male unites with female for procreation, the pleasure experienced is held to be due to nature. But males with males or females with females is against nature and an outrage of the first order" (*Laws* 636c).[100]

New Testament Prohibitions

The two NT same-sex prohibitions appear in a catalog of vices against which Jews and non-Jews alike spoke out:

> Do not be deceived! Neither the sexually immoral, nor idolaters, nor adulterers, nor male prostitutes (*malakoi*) nor men who have sex with men (*arsenokoitai*), nor thieves, nor the greedy, nor drunkards, nor slanderers, nor swindlers will inherit the kingdom of God. (1 Cor 6:9–10 AT)

> The law is not established for the law-abiding person but for the law-defying ... the sexually immoral, men who have sex with men (*arsenokoitai*), slave-traders, liars, perjurers and whatever else is contrary to the sound doctrine that conforms to the glorious gospel. (1 Tim 1:10 AT)

---

been questioned, given Nero's intense feelings for and eventual marriage to Poppaea Sabina. *Encyclopaedia Britannica*, 15th ed., s.v. "Nero."

99. Ryan, "Lex Scantinia," 159–62. The AD sixth-century Justinian law code explicitly legislated against homosexual practitioners with death as the penalty (*Institutes* 4, 18, 2–3 *Corpus Iurus Civilis*).

100. Plato's language is identical to that of Paul's in Rom 1:26–27, 1 Cor 6:9–10, and 1 Tim 1:10.

1 Corinthians 6:9–10

The 1 Cor 6:9–10 prohibitions are distinctive in specifying four (if not five) sexual practices that exclude one from the kingdom of God. The first *pornoi* is commonly translated as "the sexually immoral" (ESV, NIV, NET) or "fornicators" (KJV, NKJV, NASB, NASU, NRSV). The Greek root *porn-* originally had to do with prostitution.[101] Jewish men were not to marry a woman who had been degraded by prostitution (Lev 21:14 LXX). Israel's lack of repentance is compared to the brazenness of a street woman who spurned the usual fees (Jer 3:3; Ezek 16:31 LXX). Hence, some translate the Greek term as "whoremongers" (MRD, YLT). But by Paul's day, *pornoi* encompassed a wide range of heterosexual vices, including adultery (e.g., 1 Cor 6:9), casual sex (1 Cor 7:1–2; 1 Thess 4:3), street prostitution (1 Cor 6:15–18), cult prostitution (Rev 2:14, 20; compare 1 Cor 6:9), and incest (1 Cor 5:1).

The second prohibition is normally translated "idolaters." But since it is flanked by sexual sins, it could readily be understood as cult prostitutes. Religious prostitution is amply documented throughout antiquity. Mosaic law stipulated that "no Israelite woman shall be a cult prostitute (*pornē*), nor shall any Israelite man be a cult prostitute" (*porneuōn*, LXX Deut 23:17–18). Also, "to play the harlot" (*porneuōmen*) was a familiar phrase for engaging in idolatry. Paul himself used it to describe the idolatrous actions of the wilderness generation in building the golden calf (1 Cor 10:8).[102]

---

101. A πορνειον was a brothel, a πορνη a prostitute, and a πορνικος τελος the tax paid by brothel-keepers. LSJ, πορνεια, 1450.

102. Hauck, "Πόρνη," 581–85.

"Adulterers" (*moichoi*) are listed third. The Greek term is a common one for infidelity in the marriage relationship (Luke 18:11; Heb 13:4). It was also frequently used as a metaphor for Israel's unfaithfulness to God. Jeremiah, for example, spoke of Jerusalem's "adulteries" (*moicheia*) and "shameless prostitutions (*tēs porneias*) on the hills of the countryside" (Jer 13:27; cf. Wis.14:26).

The fourth and fifth prohibitions are male specific. The latter of these, *arsenokoitai*, is clearer than the former *malakoi*. The word *arsenokoitai* is a compound of two terms which, when joined together in this way, mean "men who bed men," a common euphemism for sexual relations.[103] Although the exact compound is not found prior to Paul, the uncompounded words in contexts having to do with same-sex relations can be readily found.[104] In fact, the parallel with Lev 18:22 and 20:13—*arsenos koitēn*—is hard to miss.[105] One can even go so far as to say that Paul is drawing directly on these two texts. For the only time Paul uses *arsēn* is when he is recalling the Septuagintal term for "male" (Rom 1:27; Gal. 3:28; 1 Cor 6:9; 1 Tim 1:10; compare Gen 1:27; Lev 18:22).[106] And the language of "males who

103. In comparable compounds -*koitēs* has a verbal force, and the first element specifies the object of the verbal action. So *arsenokoitai* should be translated "those who sleep with men" as opposed to "men who sleep around." BDF §109.

104. See, for example, Lev 18:22; 20:13; Num 31:17–18; Judg 21:11–12; Philo, *Abr.* 135–36; LSJ 246–47.

105. For further discussion, see Wright, "Homosexuals or Prostitutes?" 125–53. Compare *Anthologia Graeca Epigram* 9.686 where it is said that prefect Basil, who defeated the forces of Babylon, was not frightened of the barbarian nor of men who share their beds with men (*ouk arrenas arrenokoitas*).

106. With few exceptions *arsēn* and the variant spelling *arrēn* are only found in the first seven books of the LXX.

bed males" appears in the Septuagint only in Lev 18:22 and 20:13. This is an important point, for it renders invalid any claim that because the term first occurred in Paul, we cannot be sure of its meaning. The fact of the matter is that Paul coined other compounds to describe Gentile vices. For instance, the second vice, "idolatry" (*eidōlolatria*)—a compound of "idol" (*eidōlon*) and "worship" (*latreia*)—also first appears in Paul's writings. Yet no one disputes its connection with the OT prohibitions of the worship of idols or understands it to mean anything else.[107]

Some take issue with translating *arsenokoitai* as "males who bed males," claiming that Paul was targeting a mentor-student relationship said to be common in Greco-Roman educational circles. The claim, however, has several difficulties. First, upper-class educated Greeks were a distinct minority in the typical first-century congregation. Slaves and the lower classes are addressed for the most part (1 Cor 1:26; 7:21; 1 Tim 6:1; Titus 2:9; 1 Pet 2:18). Second, the relationship between a student and his mentor bears little resemblance to current Western pedophilia. The Greek mentor-student relationship was consensual. The mentor was "lover" (*erastēs*) and the student "beloved" (*erōmenos*). Third, the teacher-student relationship was not in principle an erotic one. The student was loved for his beautiful mind, passionate intelligence, and noble character (Plato *Lovers* 132a; *Laws* 836a).[108] Greek

---

107. Büchsel, "εἰδωλολάτρης," 379–80.

108. Plato comments, "I entered the grammar school of the teacher Dionysius and saw there the young men [students] who are accounted the most handsome and of distinguished family, and their lovers [teachers/mentors]. Now it chanced that two of the young people were disputing . . . about Anaxagoras [Ionian philosopher] or about

educators and philosophers viewed "lust of the flesh" as disgraceful. A mentor who "craves the body rather than the soul" was considered dishonorable, and a student who used sexual favors to gain standing or money was deemed shameful (Plato *Banquet* 183c–e). Intimacy was limited to expressions of gratitude toward a mentor for making one "wise and good." "Only then and there and in no other case can a student honorably indulge his lover"; those of any other sort were said to be "disgraceful" (Plato *Banquet* 183c-e). Such indulgences did not include intercourse. Chaste relationships were the ideal. Plato comments, "He that counts bodily desire as secondary ... with soul lusting really for soul, regards the bodily satisfaction of the body as an outrage, and, reverently worshipping temperance, courage, nobility and wisdom, will desire to live always chastely in company with the chaste object of his love" (Plato *Laws* 8.836c–d).

There are those who restrict the meaning of *arsenokoitai* both here and in 1 Tim 1:10 to "lovers of boys" and claim that Paul is prohibiting the first-century equivalent of pedophilia. But, if this were the case, Paul would have used the familiar Greek term *paiderastiai*—"lovers of boys," which had to do with men keeping young boys for their sexual pleasure.[109] Plato states, "They are boy-lovers (*paiderastousi*) and have no natural interest in wiving and getting children ... a lover of boys (*paiderastēs*) or the willing mate of a man (*philerastēs*)" (*Banquet* 192b). "Against

---

Oenopides [geometer and astronomer]." Plato *Lovers* 132a; cf. *Laws* 836a.

109. The Greek term παιδεραστια is a compound of "child" (παις) and "lover" (ἐραστια). LSJ 1286.

this love of boys (*paiderastiai*) a law should have been enacted" (*Banquet* 181d).

However, the Greek term for "boy lover" is not found in Paul's writings. Nor does it appear elsewhere in the Greek Bible. Instead, Paul uses the Greek word for an adult male (*arsēn*), bed (*koitē*), and the suffix that denotes a masculine agent (*-tēs*).[110] When one puts all three together, the result is "an adult male who has coitus with another adult male" (*arsenokoitēs*). This is exactly the kind of activity Philo mentions, when speaking of Sodom: "Those who were men mounted one another" (*andres ontes arresin epibainontes*, *Abr.* 135–36), and it is identical to what is found in Lev 18:20 (*meta arsenos koitēn*), Lev 20:23 (*meta arsenos koitēn*), and a wide range of Jewish, Greek, and Romans authors.

Some suppose that *arsenokoitai* has the meaning "abusers of males." Yet this does not really fit the sexual grouping in 1 Cor 6:9, for it assumes that it is not the act itself but its excess that is wrong. This would make "sexual immorality," "idolatry," and "adultery" equally acceptable as long as one did not overdo it. Certain English translations render *arsenokoitai* as "abusers of themselves with men" or "male prostitutes" (ASV, KJV, TNT, WEB, DBY). But while the term *arsenokoitai* could be stretched to refer

---

110. See ἄρσην (variant spelling ἄρρην) in LSJ (1) *the male sex* (2) *masculine, strong*; metaph. *mighty*; also ἄρρην male, of the male sex, opposite θῆλυς (*female*); substantivally τὸ ἄρσην *(the) male sex* (Matt 19:4; Rev 12:5; Rom 1:27). See also κοίτη (1) generally *bed* (Luke 11:7); specifically *marriage bed* (Heb 13:4); (2) euphemistically *sexual intercourse*, κοίτη ἡ, (κεῖμαι) = κοῖτος; plural *sexual excesses, promiscuity, illicit affairs* (Rom 13:13); (3) idiomatically κοίτην ἔχειν literally *have bed*, i.e., to have intercourse (Rom 9:10). For the suffix -της, see BDF §109.8.

to those who pay for sex, it cannot refer to those who provide it. The Greek ending *-tēs* refers to those who seek out a same-sex partner.[111]

Paul's fourth sexual vice, *malakoi*, is unique to the Corinthian vice list: "Neither the sexually immoral, nor idolaters (perhaps cult prostitutes), nor adulterers, nor *malakoi*, nor *men who bed men* will inherit the kingdom of God" (1 Cor 6:9–10). Because *malakoi* appears as a noun only here in the Greek Bible, it is difficult to pin down the meaning. The Greek adjective *malakos* ranges in meaning from "soft" and "delicate" to "weak" and "cowardly."[112] So translations are wide ranging. They include "catamites" (JB), "male prostitutes" (NIV, TNIV, NCV, HCSB, NLT, NRSV), "boy prostitutes" (NAB), "the effeminate" (ASV, KJV, NASV, Phillips), "weaklings" (TNT, Luther), "perverts" (CEV), "homosexuals" (NKJV), "passive homosexual partners" (NET), and "those who make women of themselves" (DBY).[113]

A common understanding is that *malakoi* and *arsenokoitai* denote passive and active partners in a same-sex

---

111. There are a number of Greek verbs for those who abuse others, such as *kakoucheō, kataponeō, atimazō, epēreazō, hybrizō,* and *exoudeneō*), but *koitizō* is not one of them.

112. "The words of a whisperer are like *soft* (*malakoi*) morsels" (Prov 26:22); "With patience a ruler may be persuaded, and a *soft* (*malakos*) tongue will break a bone (Prov 25:15); "Why then did you go out? To see a man clothed in *soft* (*malakos*) clothing?" (Matt 11:8; Luke 7:25). See LSJ, "μαλακός" [1] softness, delicacy, effeminacy [2] want of patience, weakness (1076–77).

113. Some translations render *malakoi* and *arsenokoitai* with a single word or phrase such as *homosexuals* (NKJV), *men who practice homosexuality* (ESV), *sexual perverts* (REB), or *homosexual perversion* (TEV, NEB).

relationship. This is reflected in the JB's "catamites and sodomites" and the NET's "passive homosexual partners and practicing homosexuals."[114] The difficulty is the lack of parallels in Paul's day. *Malakoi* and *arsenokoitai* is not the language of same-sex partners. "Lover" (*erastēs*) and "beloved" (*erōmenos*) are the first-century terms. And since "lover" and "beloved" fought side by side on the battlefield, they hardly fit a passive-active pairing—the *malak-* word group being used of those who lacked courage and strength. For example, "the Athenians' ancestral boast in war," states Demosthenes, "is to yield to none and conquer all, renouncing through indolence and cowardice (*malakian*) the deeds of their ancestors and the interests of their fatherland (*Answer to Philip's Letter* 11.22). And Plutarch comments that "the soldiers of Lucius Vitellius were more experienced and used to hard work, whereas Roman Emperor Otho's men had become "soft" (*malakoi*, *Otho* 5.5.1–3).

Nor could the "beloved" adolescent of the Greek mentor be described as a *malakos*. This is because Greeks did not look on adolescents as "weak" or "soft." Strength and courage were valued in adolescent and adult males alike. Xenophon contrasts those marked by "dainty elegance" (*malakiai*) with those who demonstrate "physical strength, manly courage and sobriety" (*Banquet* 8.1.8).

---

114. L&N μαλακός §88.281 "the passive male partner in homosexual intercourse; as in Greek, a number of other languages also have entirely distinct terms for the active and passive roles in homosexual intercourse" and §88.280 "it is possible that ἀρσενοκοίτης in certain contexts refers to the active male partner in homosexual intercourse in contrast with μαλακός, the passive male partner."

"Transvestites" is a possible translation. *Malakoi* was used of men who affected to be women and attired themselves accordingly. Cross-dressing was a cultural reality as early as the Canaanites. It motivated the Mosaic prohibition, "A woman must not wear men's clothing, nor a man wear women's clothing, for the Lord your God detests anyone who does this" (Deut 22:5). Transvestism was found in Greco-Roman artistic circles. A papyrus text dated 245 BC refers to a dancer from the theater district, whose attire would be characterized as "feminine" rather than masculine: "Send me also Zenobius *ton malakon* with a drum and cymbals and castanets, for he is wanted by the women for the sacrifice; let him wear as fine clothes as possible."[115]

"Male prostitutes" is also a possibility.[116] *Malakoi* was used of those who played the part of a woman for pay or profit of some kind. Pimps and male prostitutes were a social phenomenon in Paul's day, much as they are today. Demosthenes used the *malak-* word grouping of one Pausanias, "a whoremonger (*pornō*)," because, "although he swaggers like a man, he *allows himself to be used like a woman* and submits to degenerates" (*Letters* 4.11). Plato did the same: "Will they not likewise reproach that man who plays the woman's part (*tēn malakian*) with the resemblance he bears to his model? Is there any man, then, who will ordain by law a practice like that? Not one, I should say, if he has a notion of what true law is" (*Laws* 836e).

Of the two possibilities, "male prostitutes" best fits the Corinthian cultural context. The term "to corinthianize" was coined early on to highlight the city's investment

115. Compare the translation "the effeminate" in the ASV, KJV, NASB, and Phillips.

116. NIV, TNIV, NCV, HCSB, NLT, and NRSV.

in the retail of sexual pleasures, since the city was strategically located as a getaway for mariners and travelers. It further fits the social attitudes of the day. Men of social standing regarded male prostitution as the ultimate act of human degradation. To do so was, in Greek opinion, to "stoop to the level of an 'animal.'" This was true regardless of whether the sexual favors were motivated by money, public favor, or patronage. Plato thought the same: "When male unites with female for procreation the pleasure experienced is held to be due to nature. But males with males or females with females is against nature and an outrage of the first order" (*Laws* 636c).

1 Timothy 1:9–11

The second NT same-sex prohibition also appears in a catalog of vices: "The law is not established for the law-abiding person but for the law-defying . . . those who strike down fathers and mothers, men slayers, the sexually immoral (*pornoi*), men who have sex with men (*arsenokoitai*), slave traders, liars, perjurers—and whatever else is contrary to the sound doctrine that conforms to the glorious gospel" (1 Tim 1:9–11 AT). The Corinthian *malakoi* is conspicuously absent. In fact, only two of the five Corinthian sexual vices are found among the prohibitions.

The broader context has to do with false teaching. Timothy is urged five verses earlier to "command certain people not to teach false doctrines any longer." One piece of the false teaching included improper use of the OT law (vv. 7–11). Paul is emphatic in insisting that anyone who promotes any of the acts listed here not only breaks the law but also promotes doctrine not in conformity with the gospel.

The Same-Sex Challenge

Three things are to be noted about these acts. First, Paul takes the latter six of the Ten Commandments and contextualizes them for a Greco-Roman society. Those who dishonor mother and father become "those who strike down fathers and mothers." Murderers become "man slayers" (v. 9). Adulterers become the *pornoi* and *arsenokoitai*. Those who steal become "slave traders," that is, those who traffic in human beings. Those who bear false testimony become "liars and perjurers" (v. 10).

Translations of *pornoi* with a few exceptions boil down to "the sexually immoral"[117] or "fornicators,"[118] while translations of *arsenokoitai* are some variation of "men who have sex with men."[119] The KJV's rendering of *pornoi* as "whoremongers" is without foundation (cf. "fornicators" in 1 Cor 6:9). The CEV's "sexual perverts" is equally so. The NIV is distinctive in translating the pairing as "adulterers and perverts." Since *pornoi* by NT times encompassed a wide range of heterosexual vices, something more inclusive than "adulterers" is needed. The TNIV's change to "the sexually immoral" is more in keeping with the lexical possibilities of *pornoi* both here and in 1 Cor 6:9. The NIV's translation of *arsenokoitai* as "perverts" is equally difficult. The TNIV's change to "men who practice homosexuality" is an improvement. But Murdoch's "males who copulate with males" is exactly the sense of the Greek.

As noted earlier, *arsenokoitai* is a combination of the Greek masculine suffix denoting agency (*-tēs*), the word

---

117. See, for example, the HCSB, TNIV, RSV, ESV, NAB, NET, NLT, NASB, and NCV.

118. See, for example, the ASV, NKJ, and NRSV.

119. See, for example, the NKJV, RSV, NRSV, ESV, TNIV, NLT, NAB, NET, MRD, NCV, and CEV.

for "bed" (*koitē*), and the term for "male" (*arsēn*), which, when joined together in this way, means "men who *bed* men"—a common euphemism for sexual relations.[120] Some translate *arsenokoitai* as "homosexuals" both here and in 1 Cor 6:9.[121] It is best, however, to include a term such as "practicing" to distinguish it from those who struggle with same-sex attraction but do not give in to such urges. In order to avoid anachronism, it is also best to specify "males." The term *arsenokoitai* is not a gender-inclusive one. So translations such as "sexual relations with people of the same sex" (NCV) would not be accurate.

The second thing to observe is that all these acts, including *pornoi* and *arsenokoitai*, are identified as contrary to "the Law"—God's revealed will for his people. The notion of moral standards for the Christian life is wholly consonant with the gospel. To speak of "the Good News," then, is to speak of a moral code not unlike that found in Mosaic law. "Law" is something positive, especially for society-at-large. Paul defines the Law's legitimate use as that of a social restraint—"not for the law-abiding person but for the law-defying" (v. 9). This makes its ethical norms wholly appropriate as boundary markers for the society of any day or age.

The third thing to see is that Paul goes on to say that these practices are contrary to "the sound doctrine that conforms to the glorious gospel" (v. 11). There is no pitting of Law against gospel here. Anyone who engages in

---

120. In comparable compounds -*koitēs* has a verbal force, and the first element specifies the object of the verbal action. So *arsenokoitai* should be translated "those who sleep with men" as opposed to "men who sleep around." See BDF §109.

121. See, for instance, the NASB, NASU, and HCSB.

such practices not only breaks the Law but also promotes a lifestyle at odds with the gospel. This makes the gospel not merely a message of grace, as some are wont to claim, but also a code of ethics.

SAME-SEX THEOLOGY: ROMANS 1:24–32

> Therefore God gave them over in the sinful desires of their hearts to sexual impurity for the degrading of their bodies with one another. They exchanged the truth of God for a lie, and worshiped and served created things rather than the Creator ... Because of this, God gave them over to shameful lusts. Even their women exchanged natural relations for unnatural ones. In the same way the men also abandoned natural relations with women and were inflamed with lust for one another. Men committed indecent acts with other men, and received in themselves the due penalty for their perversion ...

Romans 1:24–32 is the biblical passage that speaks most directly to the fundamental wrongness of same-sex activity. It is significant for a number of reasons. For one, its scope is transcultural. It includes both genders and not just sexual activity between men: "Women exchanged natural relations for unnatural ones ... in the same way the men abandoned natural relations with women" (vv. 26–27). It documents same-sex activity throughout history rather than at a distinct point in time: "Ever since the creation of the world ... they [human beings] became fools ... So God gave them over in the sinful desires of their hearts to sexual impurity for the degrading of their bodies with one another" (vv. 20–24). And it spells out God's universal response to this failure: "The wrath of God is revealed from heaven ... they received in themselves the due penalty for their perversion" (vv. 18, 27).

Second, Paul's teaching in Rom 1 is rooted in the biblical doctrine of creation and therefore can't be dismissed or explained away on the basis of a particular legal code or specific cultural circumstances. Paul grounds his theology in that which is intrinsic to our creation as heterosexual human beings. The key term is "nature" (*physis*). In engaging in same-sex relations, women act "against nature" (*para physin*) and men abandon their "natural function" (*tēn physikēn chrēsin*).[122]

Paul is not the only first-century writer to identify same-sex activity as "against nature." Philo calls same-sex relations "discarding the law of nature" (*ton tēs physeōs nomon*, *Abr.* 135), whereas heterosexual relations are "by the laws of nature" (*nomois physeōs*, *Spec. Laws* 3.59). Josephus identifies the only mixture of the sexes that is "according to nature" (*kata physin*) as that of a man and a woman, while the mixture of men with men is "worthy of death" (*Ag. Ap.* 2.199). In his later works, the Greek philosopher Plato labels heterosexual relations as "according to nature" (*kata physin*), even as same-sex activity is "contrary to nature" (*para physin*) and "an outrage of the first order" (*Laws* 636B–C; 836A–C; 841D–E).

It is sometimes claimed that Paul is talking not about homosexuals who behave according to their orientation but about heterosexuals who act contrary to theirs. The facts, however, are not in evidence. There is no such

122. "Natural function" (τὴν φυσικὴν χρῆσιν) is a euphemistic way of referring to sexual intimacy that is in accordance with how human beings were created. See L&N §23.65.

The Same-Sex Challenge

thing as differing orientations within the created order of things. Scripture teaches without exception that God created humankind as *heterosexual*. The only union Scripture acknowledges is where "a man shall leave his father and his mother, and shall cleave to his wife; and they shall become one flesh" (Gen 2:24 NASB). Jesus calls this union divinely ordained (Matt 19:6; Mark 10:9). Paul names it "a profound mystery" and one that bears comparison with the union of Christ and the church (Eph 5:31–32). "Let each man have his own wife, and each woman her own husband" leaves no room for same-sex unions (1 Cor 7:2).

It is important not to read a twenty-first-century mind-set back into antiquity. Paul is dealing with violations of the created order of male and female and not with violations of sexual orientation. Indeed, the distinction between heterosexual and homosexual orientations is one that a Jew with a theology of creation based on Gen 1–2 could not have. This is clear from Paul's use of the creation language of "male"(*arsēn*) instead of "man" (*anēr*) and "female" (*thēlys*) instead of "woman"—or "masculine" and "feminine" respectively.[123] They are not Paul's usual terms, used only here and in Gal 3:28. They are, rather, the language of Gen 1:27 (LXX), "male and female [*arsen kai thēly*] he created them" (compare Gen 5:2). Indeed, the only other time these terms crop up in the NT is when Gen 1:27 is cited (Matt 19:4; Mark 10:6; Gal 3:28) and created human beings as "male and female" is invoked (Matt 19:4; Mark 10:6).

A third reason Rom 1:24–32 is important is the linkage between same-sex activity and a breakdown of the

---

123. See L&N §79.102–3.

Creator-creature distinction. The key word is *exchanged*. "Since the creation of the world," human beings have "*exchanged* (*ēllaxan*) the glory of the immortal God for images made to look like a mortal human" (vv. 20–23 TNIV); "they have *exchanged* (*metēllaxan*) the truth of God for a lie and worshiped and served created things rather than the Creator" (v. 25). The same language of *exchange* is used of same-sex activity in verses 26–27. The reversal of the created order in worship is reflected in the reversal of the created order in sexuality. Women *exchanged* (*metēllaxan*) natural relations for unnatural ones (v. 26). Men did "likewise" (*homoiōs*, v. 27). Paul's point is that abandoning natural relations with the opposite sex is directly related to abandoning worship of the Creator (v. 25).

Idolatry is at the heart of this reversal. Idolatry of self instead of devotion to the Creator is the fundamental human transgression. In turning away from God, human beings turn toward "self," indulging in all forms of self-gratification and pleasuring. They reject that which is "other" in the Creator, and they reject that which is "other" in the opposite sex. Instead of acknowledging God as "the maker of heaven and earth," human beings take what is God's alone and make it their own.

Paul's starting point is God's clear revelation of himself as Creator: "Ever since the creation of the world his eternal power and divine nature . . ." (vv. 18–22 NRSV). "They [humankind] exchanged the glory of the immortal God for images resembling a mortal human being . . . They exchanged the truth about God for a lie and worshiped and served the creature" (NRSV vv. 23, 25). God's response to self-worship throughout human history has been one of righteous anger: "For God's wrath has been

The Same-Sex Challenge

revealed against every human form of godlessness and unrighteousness of those who suppress the truth [of God as Creator] through wrongdoing ... Therefore God gave them over in the sinful desires of their hearts to sexual impurity for the degrading of their bodies with one another" (vv. 18, 24 AT).

It is sometimes said that homosexuality is not freely chosen and therefore is unavoidable. Yet, Paul goes on to say just the opposite. His language is active rather than passive. Both genders are described as free agents. Men willfully abandoned (active voice) natural relations with women and opted for unnatural sexual activity with men (vv. 26–27). The language is that of consenting adults. It is not a case of "my hormones made me do it." Paul states that "men" (not boys or youth) "abandoned" natural relations with women, became "inflamed with love for one another," and then acted on that passion in very deliberate ways (vv. 27–28). And "women" (not girls or youth) consciously "exchanged" (active voice) natural for unnatural sexual activity (v. 24–26). Then too there are consequences for the choices made. Those who engage in homosexual acts are recipients of "God's wrath" (v. 18) and receive "in themselves the due penalty for their error" (v. 27).

It is true that same-sex unions are but one form of "wickedness" listed in these verses. Paul goes on to add envy, murder, strife, deceit, malice, gossip, slander, God-hatred, insolence, and arrogance (among others) as also deserving of death (vv. 28–32). On the other hand, same-sex activity is highlighted and focused on in an exceptional way. Some consequently think that Paul is addressing same-sex perversions or abuses, rather than same-sex relations per se.[124] Paul does use the language of excess: "*shameful* lusts," "*consumed* with passion," and "*indecent* acts" (vv. 26–27). But it is important to notice that what is shameful is not same-sex perversions but same-sex activity per se. Paul states in the first part of verse 26 that God "gave humanity over to dishonorable passions." He then goes on to identify these dishonorable passions with the exchange—not the abuse—of natural sexual relations for unnatural ones.

Also, the creation language of "masculine" (*arsen*) and "feminine" (*thēly*) shows that Paul is concerned with a reversal of the created order of male and female, and not with perversions or abuses of same-sex relations. It is men and women acting against their universally created nature as heterosexuals that marks the activity as "shameful" and "indecent." Women and men opted not merely for unnatural forms of sex (such as oral or anal) but for what was "against nature" (*para physin*) and sought what Paul labels as a "shameful" perversion"—coitus with the same sex.

Paul's theology is in line with the other moralists of his day. Same-sex activity was a Gentile vice uniformly abhorred by Jews and non-Jews alike. The first-century Greek historian Plutarch calls same-sex activity "indecent" (*Dialogue On Love* 751D–752B), while the first-century Jewish historian Josephus states, "Our laws [about marriage] own no other mixture of the sexes but that which

---

124. It is sometimes said that Paul need only be referring to what were culturally considered perverted forms of heterosexual activity such as anal and oral sex. But the force of the comparative "likewise the men" at v. 27, where Paul states that "men abandoned natural relations with women and were inflamed with lust for one another," points to same-sex activity for women as well.

nature has appointed (*kata physin*), of a man with his wife ... But it abhors the mixture of a male with a male (*tēn pros arrenas arrenōn estygēken*) and if anyone do that, death is his punishment" (*Ag. Ap.* 2.25).

This is not to say that same-sex activity is a greater wrong than others. What it does say, however, is that Paul sees it as a more fundamental wrong in that it strikes at what is intrinsic to our humanness. In highlighting same-sex activity, Paul transcends the cultural forms of a particular point in time and addresses the foundational issue of human sexuality as created and intended by God—the creation of the human being as male and female (Gen 1:27).

Conclusion: The Way Forward

Our society is a sexually broken one. The first step forward is recognizing this fact. Instant gratification has become a part of the American way of life: fast food, designer clothes, instant credit, and quick sex. The forth-annual Sex Week took place mid-April at Northwestern University in Chicago, Illinois. The event was founded in 2007 by members of the College Feminists to provide "an open forum for the discussion of sexuality." More than one thousand students attend workshops, enticed by slogans such as "Let's get it on" and "It's coming . . . are you?" and titles such as "How to better please female sex partners." The sexual fair includes workshops for both heterosexual and homosexual partners. The theme is "Sex is everywhere, Sex Week is coming, let's get it on."[1]

This is the world we live in today, a world that revolves around the next sexual high and self-gratification event. Traditional values of commitment and self-sacrifice have become things of the past. This is due in large part to the decline of moral absolutes. We have come a long way from *Father Knows Best*, *The Andy Griffith Show*, and *The Donna Reed Show*. Families and local churches have largely abdicated their roles in providing a biblically based understanding of "the birds and the bees." Public school sex education has been reduced to instruction about health

1. College Feminists, "Sex Week Is Coming," http://groups.northwestern.edu/sexweek.

and safe-sex practices. Peer pressure overpowers parental voices. Right to privacy trumps accountability.

The lack of a moral order tears at the marital fabric of our society. The fragmentation of the extended family and the breakup of the nuclear family are large contributing factors. In many respects, marriage has become nothing more than a social contract, where two people sign on the dotted line. Marriage vows no longer include "as long as we both shall live" but "as long as we both shall love." The annual 25 percent divorce rate and multiple marriages attest to this reality. Twenty years ago, divorce carried a social stigma. Today, it is considered a civil right. The fact that the divorce rate is now higher in Christian circles than in society at large is deeply troubling. The prevailing understanding is that God owes us a marriage where our needs are met and our desires are satisfied. If our current spouse is not meeting our needs, then we have a right, and even an obligation, to find a spouse who will.

In a significant sense, marriage has been reduced to that of a civil union with all the attending rights and privileges. This is evident from the controversy surrounding same-sex marriages, where the Civil Liberties Union and names such as Mahatma Gandhi and Martin Luther King Jr. are invoked. Fifteen years ago, it was the rare family that had a relative who self-identified as gay or lesbian. Today, it is the rare family that lacks one. The issue has become a highly politicized one. In 1996, we saw the United States Congress pass the Defense of Marriage Act (DOMA), defining marriage as a union between a man and a woman, and we watched while the Circuit Court of Hawaii voided existing legislation prohibiting same-sex unions. Since then, we have seen virtually every state scramble to put

DOMA legislation in place, only to have the state courts challenge the constitutionality of that legislation. Ten years of homosexual curricular emphasis in kindergarten through eighth grade has produced a pre-teen public school population in which one of four are confused about their sexual orientation. With the "outing" of female celebrities such as Billie Jean King, Ellen Degeneres, and Rosie O'Donnell, lesbianism has become "cool." It is now the rare urban high school where girls are not seen holding hands and making out in the halls. And lesbian experimentation is in vogue on college and university campuses.

Recognizing the same-sex ministry challenges is long overdue. The legalization of same-sex marriage in five states and the support of same-sex civil unions by several prominent evangelicals make the need for dialogue urgent and the necessity to be biblically informed, critical. The ramifications for pastors, educators, and local churches have never been keener. The legality of pastors refusing to perform same-sex marriages will be challenged. Federal and state funds for our Christian educational institutions will dwindle. And local church attendance and membership of same-sex couples and their adopted children will press us.

Christian public school teachers, social workers, and mental health professionals are increasingly prohibited from offering support, counsel, or hope to those struggling with sexual-identity issues. This leaves an unprecedented opportunity for the church to step into the gap and provide honest biblical teaching and a safe haven for strugglers seeking support. Some churches are recognizing the need and hiring staff to provide care and counseling. But unless education happens in the pulpit and in the Sunday school class, the vacuum will remain. Of course, the instruction needs to be well informed. Where it has been tried in local churches, there has been significant failure, primarily due to a lack of understanding. Teaching and preaching that advocate only stopping same-sex behavior have not come to terms with the fact that the behavior is a symptom of a deeply rooted emotional brokenness and often profound despair. A support group, authentic Christian community, and therapy are key to sexual recovery. There are a number of parachurch ministries that have stepped into the gap to provide these. But the voices telling strugglers to accept homosexuality as their identity are far louder.

The church is in a unique position historically in that its guiding force is not the shifting sands of societal opinion and human inclination but the enduring truths of God's revelation. Central to the Christian faith is the revelation of God as the "Maker of heaven and earth" (*The Apostle's Creed*). The climax of God's activity as "maker" is the creation of humankind as male and female (Gen 1:27). Sexuality, therefore, is intrinsic to the makeup of the human species. This means that a proper understanding of human sexuality is tied to a proper understanding of God's creative act and the divine intent in and through this act.

What does it mean that we are created "male and female"? And what is the divinely intended context for expressing our sexuality? Scripture affirms no sexual union other than a marital, heterosexual one—a union of *differing* genders, and this despite the numerous changes in the cultural landscape. One must take seriously the innumerable times that heterosexual unions are affirmed as the creation order as well as the absolute prohibitions of *homo*sexual unions. Nor are heterosexual unions merely for the propagation of the human species. They are theologically profound. The husband and the wife "are no longer two, but one" (Mark 10:8). The marriage of a man and a woman is a union of God's own making (Matt 19:6). Even more, it is a type of the union of Christ and his church (Eph 5:31–33).

It is the violation of the created order of *hetero*sexual unions that Scripture addresses. The issue is not a prohibition of same-sex unions between men and women who by nature are heterosexual, leaving open the possibility of a divine nod toward men and women who self-identify as gay or lesbian. A biblical worldview and doctrine of creation categorically excludes the possibility of any other pairing except male and female. All human beings *by nature* are heterosexual. There is no other created nature or order.

What got us to the point of accepting "I am gay" as a person's created identity is often overlooked. Putting self ahead of community is a profound contributing factor. Rugged individualism was important to the American push westward. But what was a mindset in the 1700s and 1800s has developed into an idolatry of self today—a "what can I get out of it" mentality. The biblical ethic, however, is a rights-surrendering ethic. Christians are called to deny self (Mark 8:34), submit one to another (Eph 5:21), look to the interests of others (Phil 2:4), and even lay down their lives for one another (1 John 3:16).

In short, we are created for community. "Let us make humankind in our own image" (Gen 1:27) at its most basic level is a statement about community. The Godhead is at heart a divine community. This makes the creation of hu-

Conclusion: The Way Forward

mankind as male and female fundamentally the creation of human community. This is clear from Adam's response to the creation of Eve as "bone of my bones" and "flesh of my flesh" (Gen 2:23). It is also clear from the verdict that male alone is "not good" (Gen 2:18). The solution was to create a "partner" (NRSV; "a help meet for him," KJV). It is important to note that this partner was not another male. Human community that reflects divine community is distinctly male and female. The statements in Gen 1–2 about the created order of humankind as male and female, who "forsake" all others and "cleave" so as to become "one flesh" are unequivocal (Gen 2:24). In short, there is a moral order implicit in the Genesis accounts precisely with reference to male and female, a moral order that is affirmed without exception by God's people throughout biblical times and beyond.

This moral order speaks to the central and normative status of sexual purity to the life and ethic of the church. Wrong choices can have devastating consequences (see 2 Sam 11:9–12). If there is a moral order in the universe—as the creation accounts affirm—then to disregard that moral order is, in effect, to affirm the very disorder that led to Christ's death on the cross. And to affirm disorder is to deny the transforming power of God that was unleashed by Christ's death and resurrection. "If anyone is in Christ," Paul states, "that person is a new creation" (2 Cor 5:17). That "new creation" includes our sexuality.

I'm often asked if we aren't being unfair to those struggling with same-sex attraction. "They can't help it" and "they can't change" are often what I hear. What is forgotten is that God requires that we say "no" to temptation. And we are empowered by the Holy Spirit to do so. Even if it could be shown that a same-sex attraction is genetically based—or perhaps a genetic flaw resulting from the fall (Gen 3), since this was not the divine intent from the beginning—that would not make same-sex activity morally right. Propensity does not legitimize any behavior, be it heterosexual or homosexual.

I also hear from those struggling with sexual sin (whether heterosexual or homosexual) that they have tried a support group or have gone to a therapist but neither helped. Community is important and group accountability is critical. But without the will to say "no" and to confess sin when we stumble, there can be no growth toward sexual wholeness. "I tried but it [therapy/support group] didn't help" likewise ignores the power of the indwelling Spirit to say "no" to sinful desires. "Do you not know," says Paul, "that your body is a temple of the Holy Spirit, who is in you, whom you have received from God?" (1 Cor 6:19). God's goal for us is to be ever more transformed into the likeness of his Son, Jesus Christ: "And we, who with unveiled faces all reflect the Lord's glory, are being transformed into his [Christ's] likeness with ever-increasing glory, which comes from the Lord, who is the Spirit" (2 Cor 3:18). Drawing on the power of God's Spirit to say "no" is critical to this transformation.

This is not to say that sexual maturity is instantaneous. On the contrary, it is a lifelong process. The Apostle Paul makes this clear in 2 Cor 4:12, "Life is *at work in* you," and in 4:16, "while the outward person wastes away, *renewal* of the inward person *increases* day by day." This renewal is accomplished by the Spirit, who sets in motion in the believer a regenerative overhaul that culminates in complete transformation at Christ's return (2 Cor 1:22; 5:5).

Conclusion: The Way Forward

Nor is the Spirit's work in us automatic or easy. It is with good cause that Paul calls the Philippian believers to work out their salvation with fear and trembling (Phil 2:12). To be sure, God is at work in us (Phil 2:13). But we must also be at work, willing ourselves to say "no" to temptation. The "no" language of the NT offers no compromise: "Put off," (Eph 4:22), "put to death" (Col 3:5), and "flee" (1 Cor 6:18) brook no resistance. Discipline and self-control are assumed in the process of transformation. Without these there can be no spiritual growth (1 Cor 9:24–27; 1 Tim 4:7–8).

The bottom line is that God's word demands certain standards of behavior from us. Whether we are a widow or widower, never married or married, engaged or single, divorced or separated, we are commanded as Christians to live out our sexuality in a manner that is "holy and honorable" (1 Thess 4:4) Outside of a heterosexual marriage, we are unequivocally called to sexual abstinence. Inside, we are called to a relationship of mutual submission and mutual respect regarding matters of sex. Outside of a heterosexual marriage, we are called to celibacy. There is no middle ground.

The need for believers to be salt and light in our communities and in our world has never been greater. Our highly mobile society makes the propagation of traditional values through the extended family and the local community a near impossibility. Christians must therefore lead the way in educating couples about their sexual responsibilities, in modeling healthy marriages, and in teaching sexual abstinence outside of marriage. It is also our responsibility to make God's standard of holiness clear to believers living outside the boundaries of what is sexually permissible. This involves a call for repentance in the case of sexual sin and holding one another accountable for living lives of sexual purity. It also involves reaching out to those who have succumbed to a sexually destructive lifestyle, supporting those who desire to change, and proclaiming the power of God to transform lives in and through it all.

Bibliography

Abel, David. "Same-Sex Marriage Bills Gain in N. E." *Boston Globe*, March 24, 2009. http://www.boston.com/news/local/vermont/articles/2009/03/24/same_sex_marriage_bills_gain_in_ne/.

Adkins-Regan, E. "Sex Hormones and Sexual Orientation in Animals." *Psychobiology* 16 (1988) 335–47.

Allo, Ernest-Bernard. *Seconde Epitre aux Corinthiens*. 2nd ed. Paris: J. Gabalda, 1956.

Associated Press. "House Kills Bid to Void Clinton Gay Bias Order." *Los Angeles Times*, August 6, 1998. http://articles.latimes.com/keyword/executive-orders/featured/3.

Bahlburg, H. Meyer. "Sex Hormones and Male Homosexuality in Comparative Perspective." *Archives of Sexual Behavior* 6 (1977) 297–325.

Bailey, D. Sherwin. *Homosexuality and the Western Christian Tradition*. London: Longmans & Green, 1955.

Bailey, J. Michael. *The Man Who Would Be Queen: The Science of Gender-Bending and Transsexualism*. Washington DC: Joseph Henry, 2003.

Bailey, J. Michael, and R. C. Pillard. "A Genetic Study of Male Sexual Orientation." *Archives of General Psychiatry* 48 (1991) 1089–96.

Bailey, J. Michael, et al. "Heritable Factors Influence Sexual Orientation in Women." *Archives of General Psychiatry* 50 (1993) 217–23.

Beeston, A. F. L. "One Flesh." *Vetus Testamentum* 36 (1986) 117.

Belleville, Linda L. "Facts and Fictions about Homosexuality: Debunking the Socio-Biblical Myths of the Religious Gay Community." *Cultural Encounters: A Journal for the Theology of Culture* 2 (2005) 65–86.

———. *Women Leaders and the Church*. Grand Rapids: Baker Academic, 2000.

Bissette, David C. "Internet Pornography Statistics." September, 2003. http://www.internetfilterreview.com/internet-pornography-statistics.html.

Blair, Ralph. "The Bible is an Empty Closet." *Whosoever* 3 (1998). http://www.whosoever.org/v3i3/closet.html.

The Book of Common Prayer and Administration of the Sacraments and Other Rites and Ceremonies of the Church, Together With the Psalter or Psalms of David, According to the Use of The Episcopal Church. USA Edition. New York: Church Hymnal Corporation, 1979.

Brueggemann, Walter. "Of the Same Flesh and Bone (GN 2,23a)." *Catholic Biblical Quarterly* 32 (1970) 532–42.

Büchsel, Friedrich. "Εἰδωλολάτρης." In *TDNT* 2:379–80.

Byne, William, and Bruce Parsons. "Human Sexual Orientation: The Biological Theories Reappraised." *Archives of General Psychiatry* 50 (1993) 228–39.

Cantarella, Eva. *Pandora's Daughters*. Baltimore: Johns Hopkins University Press, 1987.

Carey, Benedict. "Straight, Gay, or Lying? Bisexuality Revisited." New York Times, July 5, 2005, Health section. http://www.nytimes.com/2005/07/05/health/05sex.html.

Centers for Disease Control and Prevention. "HPV Vaccine Information For Young Women." http://www.cdc.gov/std/hpv/STDFact-HPV-vaccine-young-women.htm (accessed March 10, 2010).

———. "Genital HPV Infection–CDC Fact Sheet." http://www.cdc.gov/STD/HPV/STDFact-HPV.htm (accessed March 10, 2010).

———. "Male Latex Condoms and Sexually Transmitted Diseases." http://www.cdc.gov/nchstp/od/condoms.pdf (accessed March 10, 2010).

———. "Trends in HIV- and STD-Related Risk Behaviors Among High School Students—United States, 1991–2007." http://www.cdc.gov/mmwr/about.html.

Cicero, Marcus Tullius. "In Defense of Cluentius." In *The Speeches*. Translated by H. Grose Hodge. LCL. Cambridge, MA: Harvard University, 1927.

Clark, Elizabeth A. "Sexuality." In *Encyclopedia of Early Christianity*, edited by E. Ferguson et al., 843–45. New York: Garland, 1988.

Conzelmann, Hans. *1 Corinthians*. Translated by James W. Leitch. Philadelphia: Fortress, 1981.

Crary, David. "Gay-to-Straight Therapy Repudiated by Psychologists." *South Bend Tribune*, August 6, 2009.

Crewdson, J. "Study on 'Gay Gene' Challenged." *Chicago Tribune*, June 25, 1995.

Davidson, Richard M. "Theology of Sexuality in the Song of Songs: Return to Eden." *Andrews University Seminary Studies* 27 (1989) 1–19.

De Lacoste-Utamsing, C., and K. L. Holloway. "Sexual Dimorphism in the Human Corpus Callosum." *Science* 216 (1982) 1431–32.

Diagnostic and Statistical Manual of Mental Disorders. 4th ed. Washington DC: American Psychiatric Association, 2000.

Eckert, E., et al. "Homosexuality in Monozygotic Twins Reared Apart." *British Journal of Psychiatry* 148 (1986) 421–25.

Ehrhardt, A. A., and H. F. Meyer-Bahlburg. "Effects of prenatal sex hormones on gender-related behavior." *Science* 211 (1981) 1312–18.

Famighetti, Robert, ed. "Vital Statistics." In *The World Almanac and Book of Facts 1997*. Mahwah, NJ: World Almanac Books.

Feder, H. "Hormones and Sexual Behavior." *Annual Review of Psychology* 35 (1984) 165–200.

Freeman, Paul. "Chapter 60." *Sexual Offences Act of 1967*. London: Controller's Library, 1967. http://www.opsi.gov.uk/acts/acts1967/pdf/ukpga_19670060_en.pdf.

Fryling, Alice. "Why Wait for Sex? A Look at the Lies We Face." *Student Leadership Journal* 7 (1995) 1. http://www.intervarsity.org/studentsoul/item/why-wait.

Gagnon, Robert. *The Bible and Homosexual Practice: Texts and Hermeneutics*. Nashville: Abingdon, 2001.

Genung, Mike. "How Many Porn Addicts are in Your Church?" www.crosswalk.com/faith/pastors/1336107.html.

Gerstenberger, E. "ידע." In *TDOT* 2:1051–55.

Gordon, Richard. "A Critical Review of the Physics and Statistics and their Role in Individual versus Societal Survival of the AIDS Epidemic." *Journal of Sex and Marital Therapy* 15 (1989) 5–30.

Gotestam, K. O., et al. "Handedness, Dyslexia and Twinning in Homosexual Men." *International Journal of Neuroscience* 63 (1992) 179–86.

Green, R. *Sissy Boy Syndrome and the Development of Homosexuality*. New Haven, CT: Yale University Press, 1987.

Grenfell, B. P., et al. *The Oxyrhynchus Papyri*. 42 vols. London: Egypt Exploration Fund, 1898–1974. http://www.papyrology.ox.ac.uk/POxy/VExhibition/images/2891.jpg.

Grudem, Wayne. *Evangelical Feminism: A New Path to Liberalism?* Wheaton, IL: Crossway, 2006.

———. "The Key Issues in the Manhood-Womanhood Controversy." In *Building Strong Families*, edited by Dennis Rainey, 29–90. Wheaton, IL: Crossway, 2002.

Haldeman, Douglas. "Gays, Ex-Gays, Ex-Ex-Gays—Examining Key Religious, Ethical and Diversity Issues." American Psychological Association Annual Meeting, August 7, 2000, Washington, DC.

Hamer, D. H., et al. "A Linkage between DNA Markers on the X-Chromosome and Male Sexual Orientation." *Science* 261 (1993) 321–27.

———. "Linkage between Sexual Orientation and Chromosome Xq28 in Males But Not in Females." *Nature Genetics* 11 (1995) 248–56.

Hamilton, Victor. *The Book of Genesis. Chapters 1–17*. Grand Rapids: Eerdmans, 1990.

Harrison, R. K. "Know." In *The International Standard Bible Encyclopedia*, edited by Geoffrey W. Bromiley. 4 vols. Grand Rapids: Eerdmans, 1979–1988.

Hauck, Friedrich. "Πόρνη." In *TDNT* 6:581–85.

Jones, David W. "Egalitarianism and Homosexuality: Connected or Autonomous Ideologies?" *JBMW* 8 (2003) 5–19.

Jones, Elise F., and Jacqueline Darroch Forrest. "Contraceptive Failure Rates Based on the 1988 NSFG." *Family Planning Perspectives* 24 (1992) 12–19.

Jones, Stanton, and Mark Yarhouse. *Homosexuality: The Use of Scientific Research*. Downers Grove, IL: InterVarsity, 2000.

———. "Science and the Ecclesiastical Homosexuality Debates." *Christian Scholar's Review* 26 (1997) 446–77.

Joy, Donald. *Bonding: Relationships in the Image of God*. Waco: Word, 1985.

Kaiser Health News. "FDA Announces Approval of HPV Vaccine Gardasil." June 9, 2006. http://www.kaisernetwork.org/daily_reports/rep_index.cfm?DR_ID=37807.

Kaiser, Wendi. "Questions on Dating & Sex." *Cornerstone Magazine* 117 (1999) 45, 47–48. http://www.askwendi.com/article.cfm?ArticleID=16.

Kallmann, K. "Comparative Twin Study on the Genetic Aspects of Male Homosexuality." *Journal of Nervous and Mental Disease* 115 (1952) 137–59.

King, M., and F. McDonald. "Homosexuals Who are Twins: A Study of Forty-Six." *British Journal of Psychiatry* 160 (1992) 407–9.

Bibliography

Kirchheimer, Sid. "Herpes Down; Other STDs Increasing." http://www.webmd.com/sexual-conditions/news/20040308/herpes-down-other-stds-increasing.

Lalumière, M. L., et al. "Sexual Orientation and Handedness in Men and Women: A Meta-Analysis." *Psychological Bulletin* 126 (2000) 575–92.

Lane, William. *Hebrews 9–13*. WBC 47b. Waco: Word, 1991.

Law Students for Reproductive Justice. "Abstinence-Only Education." http://lsrj.org/documents/09_Abstinence_Only_Education.pdf.

Lawrence v. Texas, March, 26, 2003, #02-102. http://www.supremecourt.gov/oral_arguments/argument_transcripts/02-102.pdf.

LeVay, Simon. "A Difference in Hypothalamic Structure Between Heterosexual and Homosexual Men." *Science* 258 (1991) 1034–37.

———. "Sexual Orientation: The Science and its Social Impact," forthcoming in *Reverso*. http://members.aol.com/_ht_a/slevay/page12.html.

Lindenfield, Gael. *The Emotional Healing Strategy: A Recovery Guide for Any Setback, Disappointment or Loss*. New York: Penguin, 2008.

Lindesay, J. "Laterality Shift in Homosexual Men." *Neuropsychologia* 25 (1987) 965–69.

Martin, Enos, and Ruth Keener Martin. "Developmental and Ethical Issues in Homosexuality: Pastoral Implications." *Journal of Psychology and Theology* 9 (1981) 58–68.

McCormick, C. M., and S. T. Wittlesons. "A Cognitive Profile of Homosexual Men Compared to Heterosexual Men and Women." *Psychoneuroendocrinology* 16 (1991) 459–73.

McCormick, C. M., et al. "Left-handedness in Homosexual Men and Women: Neuro-Endocrine Implications." *Psychoneuroendocrinology* 15 (1990) 69–76.

Moberly, Elizabeth. *Homosexuality: A New Christian Ethic*. Cambridge: James Clarke, 1983.

The National Institute of Allergy and Infectious Diseases. "Sexually Transmitted Infections–Human Papillomavirus and Genital Warts." www.niaid.nih.gov/factsheets/std (accessed March 10, 2010).

National Survey of Family Growth 2006–2008. "Teenagers in the United States: Sexual Activity, Contraceptive Use, and Childbearing," *Vital and Health Statistics*. Series 23, Number 30, 2008: 1–79. http://www.cdc.gov/nchs/data/series/sr_23/sr23_030.pdf.

Nicolosi, Joseph. *Reparative Therapy of Male Homosexuality: A New Clinical Approach*. Northvale, NJ: Jason Aronson Inc., 1991.

Nicolosi, Joseph, and Linda Nicolosi. *A Parent's Guide to Preventing Homosexuality*. Downers Grove, IL: InterVarsity, 2002.

Orr, Donald P., et al. "Premature Sexual Activity as an Indicator of Psychosocial Risk." *Pediatrics* 87 (1991) 141–47.

Oswalt, John. "*Bāsār*." In *TWOT* 1:136.

Parelli, Steve. "Homosexuality and the Bible," Power Point Presentation, July 27, 2007. http://www.othersheepexecsite.com/Power_Point_Presentation_on_the_Bible_and_Homosexuality.html and http://www.soulforce.org/article/homosexuality-bible (accessed March 31, 2010).

Paulk, John. *Not Afraid To Change*. Mukilteo, WA: Wine, 1998.

Radsch, Courtney C. "Teenagers' Sexual Activity Is Tied to Drugs and Drink." *New York Times*, August 20, 2004.

Risch, N., et al. "Male Sexual Orientation and Genetic Evidence." *Science* 262 (1993) 2063–65.

Rosik, Christopher. "When Therapists Do Not Acknowledge Their Moral Values: Green's Response as a Case Study." *Journal of Marital and Family Therapy* 29 (2003) 39–45.

Ryan, F. X. "The Lex Scantinia and the Prosecution of Censors and Aediles." *Classical Philology* 89 (1994) 159–62.

Saluter, Arlene, and Terry Lugaila. "Current Population Reports, Population Characteristics." Bureau of the Census. www.census.org.

Satinover, Jeffrey. *Homosexuality and the Politics of Truth*. Grand Rapids: Baker Academic, 1996.

Sexuality Information and Education Council of the United States "Knowing the Opposition." http://www.communityactionkit.org/index.cfm?pageId=920.

Skinner, John. *A Critical and Exegetical Commentary on Genesis*. New York: Charles Scribner's Sons, 1910.

Sneeringer, Christine. "Safe as a Woman." *Christian Single*, July 2001. http://www.exodus.to/content/view/248/148/.

Spitzer, Robert. "Can Some Gay Men and Lesbians Change Their Sexual Orientation?" *Archives of Sexual Behavior* 32 (2003) 403–17.

Stein, Rob. "Medical Groups Promoted Gardasil Vaccine Using Funds from Drugmaker Merck." *Washington Post*, August 19, 2009. http://www.washingtonpost.com/wp-dyn/content/article/2009/08/18/AR2009081803325.html.

Swaab, D. F., et al. "Gender and Sexual Orientation in Relation to Hypothalamic Structures." *Hormone Research* 38, suppl 2 (1992) 51–61.

Throckmorton, Warren. "Attempts to Modify Sexual Orientation: A Review of Outcome Literature and Ethical Issues." *Journal of Mental Health Counseling* 20 (1998) 283–304.

Thurston, Thomas. "Leviticus 18:22 and the Prohibition of Homosexual Acts." In *Homophobia and the Judaeo-Christian Tradition*, edited by M. L. Stemmeler and J. Michael Clark, 7–23. Dallas: Monument Press, 1990.

Tracy, Amy. "Cornered By Grace." *Focus on the Family Magazine*, March, 1998. http://www.exodus.to/content/view/246/148/.

Turner, W. J. "Homosexuality, Type 1: An Xq28 Phenomenon." *Archives of Sexual Behavior* 24 (1995) 109–34.

United States Code. "Definition of 'Marriage' and 'Spouse.'" In *Title 1 General Provisions. Chapter 1 Rules of Construction*, January 5, 2009, §7. http://uscode.house.gov/download/pls/01C1.txt.

Update: Newsletter of the Evangelical Women's Caucus 10 (1986).

U.S. Census Bureau. "Census 2000 Briefs and Special Reports." Washington: U.S. Department of Commerce Economics and Statistics Administration, 2005. http://www.census.gov/population/www/cen2000/briefs.html.

———. "Family and Living Arrangements." http://www.census.gov/population/www/socdemo/hh-fam.html.

———. "Statistical Abstract of the United States. 1995–2000." Washington: U.S. Department of Commerce Economics and Statistics Administration, 2000, section 2. http://www.census.gov/prod/www/statistical-abstract-us.html.

———. "United States Census 2000. Marriage and Divorce Data." Washington: U.S. Department of Commerce Economics and Statistics Administration, 2005. www.census.gov/main/www/cen2000.html.

———. "Vital Statistics." *Census 2000 Briefs and Special Reports*. Washington: U.S. Department of Commerce Economics and Statistics Administration, 2005.

U.S. Statistics. "Households." http://ww.infoplease.com/ipa/A0908708.html.

———. "Median Age at First Marriage, 1890–2007." http://www.infoplease.com/ipa/A0005061.html.

———. "Percent Never Married, 1970–2006." http://www.infoplease.com/ipa/A0763219.html.

Verhey, Allen. "The Holy Bible and Sanctified Sexuality—an Evangelical Approach to Scripture and Sexual Ethics." *Interpretation* 49 (1995) 41.

Ware, Bruce. "Male and Female Complementarity and the Image of God." *JBMW* 7 (2002) 14–23.

WebMD. "Modern Love: Sex & Relationships, Pornography in Relationships." December 22, 2005. http://blogs.webmd.com/sexual-health-sex-matters/2005/12/pornography-in-relationships.html.

Wenham, Gordon. *The Book of Leviticus*. NICOT. Grand Rapids: Eerdmans, 1979.

———. *Genesis 1–15*. WBC 1. Waco: Word, 1987.

———. "Homosexualität." In *Reallexikon der Assyriologie und Vorderasiatischen Archaologie*, edited by Erich Ebeling et al. 8 vols. Walter De Gruyter, 2003–2005, 4:559–68.

———. "The Old Testament Attitude to Homosexuality." *The Expository Times* 102 (1991) 359–63.

Westermann, Claus. *Genesis 1–11*. Translated by John J. Scullian. Minneapolis: Augsburg, 1981.

———. *Genesis 12–36*. Translated by John J. Scullian. Minneapolis: Augsburg, 1985.

Whitam, F. L., et al. "Homosexual Orientation in Twins: A Report on Sixty-One Pairs and Three Triplet Sets." *Archives of Sexual Behavior* 22 (1993) 187–206.

Whitehead, N. E. "Science and Homosexuality." www. http://www.mygenes.co.nz/.

Wilfong, Marsha M. "Genesis 2.18–24." *Interpretation* 42 (1988) 58–63.

Williams, T. J., et al. "Finger-Length Ratios and Sexual Orientation." *Nature* 404 (2000) 455–56.

Worthen, Anita, and Bob Davies. *Someone I Love Is Gay*. Downers Grove, IL: InterVarsity, 1996.

Wright, David. "Homosexuality." In *Encyclopedia of Early Christianity*, edited by E. Ferguson et al., 435–36. New York: Garland, 1988.

———. "Homosexuals or Prostitutes? The Meaning of *arsenokoitai* (1 Cor. 6:9, 1 Tim. 1:10)." *Vigiliae Christianae* 38 (1984) 125–53.

Yndigoyen, Rose. "*CosmoGirl!* Includes Queer Peers." August 8, 2006. www.afterellen.com.

www.ingramcontent.com/pod-product-compliance
Lightning Source LLC
Chambersburg PA
CBHW071448160426
43195CB00013B/2052